INNER BRILLIANCE

SOME KIND WORDS FOR ROS

'Working with Ros was like a breath of fresh air into my business. Although I was not 100% sure at the beginning of where it would lead or what was expected. The outcome was business changing. I reconnected deeply with my WHY, I am now able to see my business from a new perspective with a vision of where I want it to go. It also provided a platform for enhancing my website, my promotional material and best of all an alignment throughout.'
Deb Pace, Director Pacing Dynamics

'Ros takes the passion and vision you have for your business, draws out the ideas you didn't realise you had and articulates these perfectly into a document that is usable and relevant to your business to define your brand, vision, mission and values to your clients and staff.'
Cameron McKerchar, Managing Director, Tudor Insurance Australia

'I have worked with Ros on many occasions and continue to because I know the quality results she produces for my clients and for my business. Ros's work helps clients get clear on who they are, the needs of their target markets and how they wish to be positioned in the marketplace. Every chance we get, we recommend our clients see Ros first as we know it will be highly beneficial for the final client outcome.'
Ricky Verkaik, Director, Zain Digital

'Ros Weadman's passion is infectious. She turns traditional marketing on its head and provides all the tools for success based on her unique marketing code. With Ros's support, I was able to create an effective marketing plan that really works.'
Caroline Ward, Director Ki Creative

'Ros's energy and passion for communications and engagement is infectious and she really helped us as a team articulate our purpose. The groundwork that we have done here is going to be enormously beneficial in creating a Communications Team Strategy moving forward.'
Sam Shalders, Communications Team, City of Ballarat

'Finding Ros Weadman was a breath of fresh air. She listens. She gets it…Everything just works. She is professional, dedicated and timely. And she really knows her craft. Basically, I can't recommend her more highly.'
Ray Keefe, Managing Director, Successful Endeavours

'Through working with Ros, I now have a greater sense of clarity around my business message and brand differentiation.'
Khatija Halabi, Casey Hearing

'Due to the marketing activities that I am doing I am getting more leads than I ever anticipated… I highly recommend Ros to anyone that is looking to take their business to the next level.'
Andrea Jenkins, Principal Adviser, Jenbury Financial

'Ros's signature approach made us all think laterally and deeply, identifying missed marketing opportunities, and clearly defined novel approaches to take advantage of those avenues. I'd recommend this workshop to every micro to medium business owner who's frustrated with their marketing results and wants to have clear plan of action.'
Arek Rainczuk, Five Castles Portraits

'Ros's marketing masterclass provided me with so much clarity around my USP and the best way to position myself in my industry…I am now feeling so excited and motivated to take my new learnings forward in my business.'
Danielle Pooles, Dressage Plus

INNER BRILLIANCE

Build a personal brand that
amplifies your you-niqueness,
expands your influence
and elevates your worth

ROS WEADMAN

Published by Roslyn M Weadman and Global Business Publishing, a Division of Marcomms Australia 2024

ISBN: 978-0-6454388-3-3

Ebook ISBN: 978-0-6454388-4-0

Editing by The In Writing Group

Cover design and illustration by Ideas Ministry

Typesetting by BookPOD

Printed and bound in Australia by IngramSpark

 A catalogue record for this book is available from the National Library of Australia

Copyright © 2024 Roslyn M Weadman.

Roslyn M Weadman has asserted her right under the *Copyright, Designs and Patents Act 1988* to be identified as the author of this work. The information in this book is based on the author's insights, experiences, learnings and opinions.

All rights reserved. No part of this book may be reproduced, stored in or introduced into a retrieval system, or transmitted in any form or by any means (electronic, mechanical, photocopying, recording or otherwise) without written permission of the publisher and author.

This book contains general information only and does not replace specific professional advice. The publisher and author specifically disclaim any liability, loss or risk which may result from use of the information herein, nor any error or omission within the book.

'This above all: to thine own self be true.'
William Shakespeare, English playwright and poet

REAL SUPERHEROES WEAR THEIR UNDIES ON THE INSIDE ...

The superhero cape and matching mini-me doll were given to me in 2016 by my then business coach. This gift of congratulations came as a complete surprise at the end of the launch of my first book, *BrandCode – Unleash your super power through strategic marketing*.

I was just finishing my presentation when my business coach rose from the audience, came to the front of the room and presented me with the cape and doll. I burst out laughing. The doll was made in the image of the 'Super Ros' caricature created for the book. The likeness was uncanny.

The superhero cape and mini-me doll, complete with 'marketing toolbelt', were fitting for so many reasons at that time. As a public relations and marketing communications specialist for 30+ years, using the right tools and tactics were part of my daily vernacular. And, as a small business owner, I'd come to know that running a small business meant being a Jack or Jill of all trades.

But the superhero cape and mini-me doll became so much more than a metaphor for the superhero small business owner juggling multiple balls in the air. Wearing the cape and bringing the mini-me doll to workshops and speaking gigs became a great conversation starter and wonderful way of connecting with my small business owner audiences.

More than that, over time, the Super Ros character gave me confidence and a way of standing out in the marketplace. So I assumed the role and played the character. Like an actor becomes the star of the show when they put on the costume and step on to the stage, I came to think that to become a successful business person, I needed to don the Super Ros outfit and embrace the persona. And so the caricature jumped out of the book and into my business life. It was front and centre in all my branded marketing materials, including on banners, on the website, on social media.

This worked well for several years; however, as my business and I began to grow and evolve, the novelty of Super Ros began to fade. Then the epiphany happened.

For my entire career, I'd worked with hundreds of business and government leaders, building their personal brand and that of the organisation they represented. While I was the brand strategist and copywriter behind the media statements, the speeches and the marketing materials, what made my words resonate was the human being delivering them. Words can be clever, funny, sad or witty, but they only come to life because of the person who says them.

So I realised that my words too, only connected with audiences because of my passion and belief in them, combined with how I delivered the messages through my personality, body language and presence. And so my superhero cape, toolbelt and mini-me doll were relegated to the wardrobe and now only come out on special occasions.

Looking back, I find it both funny and curious that to be confident as a small business owner and shed my imposter syndrome I thought I had to be someone else, or at least communicate through my alter ego, Super Ros. And so it is for many people. They don't find it easy or comfortable to be their true selves for many reasons. They may feel insecure or unworthy, lack self-esteem, suffer from imposter syndrome or simply have never put themselves in the spotlight, preferring to champion their colleagues. Over the years, this has meant missed opportunities to progress their career, increase their salary and play a larger game.

Like the characters in movies that follow the classic hero's journey, such as Dorothy in *The Wizard of Oz*, Luke Skywalker in *Star Wars* or

Neo in *The Matrix*, you are already the hero of your own journey and have everything you need inside of you to be a success.

This is true of your personal brand. Your personal brand is not fake; it is not a superhero movie character. Your personal brand is, in fact, you!

A personal brand simply amplifies who you already are in a more intentional, aligned and consistent way. It's about getting clear on your purpose, your values, your value proposition and your zone of genius, which embodies your passions, talents, skills and specialist problem-solving intelligence. Once you have this clarity, and a strategy and structure for leverage, you can drive a more unified perception of who you are in the minds of others and shape your desired reputation.

I would like you to keep this story in mind as we begin our journey together to build you a strong personal brand and knowing that what we are unleashing – your Inner Brilliance – already exists inside of you. I'm simply your guide to help you activate, align and amplify your Inner Brilliance so you can achieve your career ambitions, business goals or leadership dreams.

To your Inner Brilliance!

Ros Weadman

This book is dedicated to those among us who dare to be brave, bold and brilliant.

I hope it inspires you to build a personal brand that unleashes your Inner Brilliance so you can leave your mark on the world.

CONTENTS

INTRODUCTION	**1**
PART 1: UNDERSTANDING PERSONAL BRANDING	**7**
The search for identity	7
Personal brand versus reputation	8
Super powers of personal branding	10
PART 2: MYTHS, TELLTALES AND LEGENDS	**17**
Myths that keep your Inner Brilliance hidden	17
Telltale signs you need a personal brand	21
Legendary personal brand lessons	27
PART 3: GOING FROM ZERO TO HERO	**33**
What unleashes Inner Brilliance?	33
Moving from invisible to influential	36
Unleashing the force within you	40
PART 4: THE INNER BRILLIANCE PERSONAL BRANDING™ SYSTEM	**45**
The system summarised	46
Purpose – Ignite your personal brand	49
Positioning – Differentiate your personal brand	68
Profile – Promote your personal brand	89
Profitability – Monetise your personal brand	123
PART 5: THE END … OR IS IT?	**143**
PS – It's only the beginning!	144
ENDNOTES	**145**
ABOUT THE AUTHOR	**149**

INTRODUCTION

'Life isn't about finding yourself. Life is about creating yourself.'
George Bernard Shaw, playwright and literary critic

What's all the fuss about?

While the term 'personal branding' may be relatively new, according to personal branding expert and professor Dr Talaya Waller, it is an age-old practice. Dr Waller surmises that 'the Theory of Personal Brand Equity is built on the heavily documented observation that humans have been building their personal brands since the beginning of trade and commerce, long before the notion of branding and brand management was introduced to the public. From an economic viewpoint, the purpose of developing a personal brand is for people to scale their value'.[1]

Personal branding is for everyone, not only for the famous, and the public domain is not an exclusive playground for celebrities. In today's 24/7 communications-technology-driven world, every person can build their personal brand and communicate their value on myriad platforms to a specific target market or a global audience.

And why not? There are clear benefits to building a personal brand. A 2019 review by Schiedt and Henseler of research conducted on personal branding found that individuals benefit from personal branding 'when competing for work, seeking advancement in specific occupations or professions, or pursuing a career path leading to higher financial earnings'[2]. Beyond the financial benefits, Gorbatov, Khapova and Lysova found that personal branding as a contemporary career technique, 'leads to greater career satisfaction, fully mediated by perceived employability'[3].

Personal branding is about defining, expressing and strategically leveraging an authentic self-identity and professional value proposition that shapes the way you want to be perceived; your reputation. Your personal brand is all-encompassing, embodying your identity, passions, values, beliefs, purpose, vision and expertise, which are invisible to the outside world. Together, these intrinsic elements influence your language, behaviour, stories, visual elements of your brand, public profile and performance results which are visible to the outside world. The iceberg graphic illustrates the interplay between the invisible and visible elements of a personal brand.

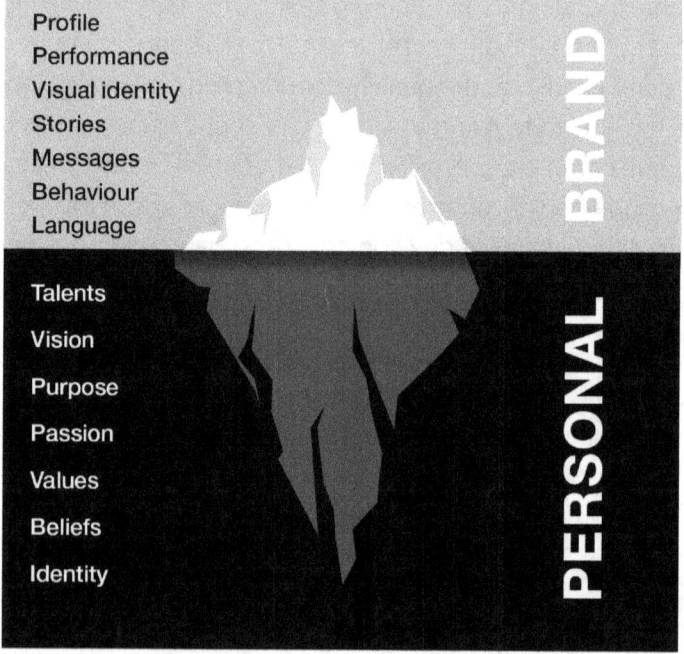

Personal Brand Iceberg ©Ros Weadman

This book will help you gain clarity and confidence in the elements below the surface, inside of you, so you can project your authentic personal brand to the outside world with volition, alignment and consistency.

Your personal brand is a bridge to your desired reputation

A strong personal brand closes the gap between your actual reputation and your desired reputation. Everyone has a reputation, but most people don't have a strong personal brand. We form an opinion about someone whether we know them well or not. This opinion is based on our collective experiences of a person, gained for example, by interacting with them directly, reading about them in a magazine, watching an interview on television, listening to a podcast, sitting in on a webinar or, vicariously, through what we've heard others say about them.

In the absence of a strong personal brand, the opinions people have about someone will vary. In effect, the reputation of people without a strong personal brand is fragmented.

People with a strong personal brand, on the other hand, build a reputation by design rather than default. Their reputation precedes them because they are known within their workplace or industry through the projection of a unified, aligned and consistent personal brand over time, in all places and on all platforms. People with a strong personal brand shape the way other people perceive them. They cultivate their desired reputation, which distinguishes them from others.

By doing so, they set themselves apart, for example, when:

- going for a more senior role
- putting forward their opinions and ideas in a meeting
- pitching for new business
- seeking media coverage.

Often, business owners, leaders, recruiters and others seek out people with a strong personal brand and particular reputation because they know the type of person they want for a role or to do business with.

So, if you want to earn a great, consistent reputation, build a strong personal brand. It's the bridge to take you from your current (possibly fragmented) reputation to your desired (cohesive) reputation.

Is personal branding really for me?

Whether you believe your existence is by chance or fate, the fact that you are one of a kind on this planet is a claim to fame worth leveraging. There is no-one else on earth with your exact passion, personality, intelligence, attitude, creativity, behaviours, habits, quirks, perceptions, perspectives, talents or core beliefs and values. Nor is there any person who has had the exact same life experiences, training or career pathway.

However, despite our you-niqueness and individual extraordinariness, most people consider themselves to be 'ordinary'. This thinking may come from not wanting to appear egotistical, self-centred, superior or arrogant. Personal branding, however, is not about trying to be superior or arrogant; it's simply about bringing out your natural passions, traits and strengths in a more intentional, aligned and consistent way. Who you are is extraordinary already. But if you step a little outside your comfort zone and let your Inner Brilliance shine, you'll step into the realm of infinite possibility, with the promise of a more extraordinary life.

Still not convinced? You're not alone

People can be held back from building a personal brand for many reasons. They may want to stay under the radar because they have a low sense of self-worth; they have what I call 'FOSO' – 'Fear of Standing Out' or they don't understand what personal branding is.

So, by staying under the radar, by not going for their dream job, by not speaking up at team meetings, by not accepting that media interview, by not wearing more colourful clothes, by not making that sales call, by not learning public presentation skills, by not <insert excuse here>, they get to stay in their comfort zone. Then later live with the regret of not acting and with that critical inner voice saying, 'I told you so!'.

What if you had a way to step out from under radar and into the light? The Inner Brilliance Personal Branding™ system will help you get out of your own way, to become your own champion and achieve all you desire in building your career, business or leadership.

Get ready to let your Inner Brilliance shine

Just as diamonds sparkle most vividly in light, a person's Inner Brilliance shines most remarkably when they project a strong, personal brand with volition. And, as a diamond without light can appear like glass, professionals who leave their personal brand to chance become commoditised among a sea of generalists.

The Inner Brilliance Personal Branding™ system is a holistic framework to define, develop, implement and manage your personal brand. It is applicable to all people across all industries and provides a step-by-step approach to build a strong authentic personal brand from scratch.

The core of the Inner Brilliance Personal Branding™ system is to bring out your 'youness'; the combination of personal attributes that makes you you-nique and the Inner Brilliance that makes a positive difference in the world like only you can. It's about tapping into what exists naturally within you and unleashing it to the world in an authentic and ecological way.

Unleashing your Inner Brilliance is like removing a cloak of invisibility. The Inner Brilliance Personal Branding™ system provides a blueprint for moving from invisible to influential. But, of course, nothing will happen if you just read the book and don't act. Like everything in life worth having, you need to take the first step and then the second and so on. You don't get fit sitting on the couch, you don't build muscle without working out, you don't change a bad habit without replacing it with a new one. It's the same with building a personal brand.

About this book

This book is written in five parts:

- **Part 1: Understanding Personal Branding** defines what it is and why it's important if you want to get ahead in today's competitive marketplace.
- **Part 2: Myths, Telltales and Legends** considers what might be holding you back from developing a personal brand and how you can overcome these challenges.
- **Part 3: Going from Zero to Hero** describes what unleashes Inner Brilliance and the journey people typically navigate in moving from invisible to influential.
- **Part 4: The Inner Brilliance Personal Branding™ System** unveils the four key outcomes of the framework – purpose, positioning, profile and profitability – and provides a step-by-step blueprint for defining, marketing and managing your personal brand.
- **Part 5: The End…or Is it?** provides a postscript message to the reader, outlining the next key step in the process.

A final word

Building a personal brand isn't a set and forget process; it's an ongoing process of learning, testing, refining and evolving. And the personal and professional rewards are well worth the investment of your time and effort.

From the moment you decide to get in the driver's seat of your personal brand, you'll start to notice that people respond to you differently. Remember, this is your journey to discover, define and amplify your strengths and qualities, and your viewpoints and ideas in a more intentional, aligned and consistent way.

Enjoy the journey and let your Inner Brilliance become your superpower.

PART 1

UNDERSTANDING PERSONAL BRANDING

'If you are not a brand, you are a commodity.'
Philip Kotler, Professor of Marketing

No longer just for celebrities, speakers, authors and others in the media spotlight, personal branding is now essential for any person who wants to stand out in today's competitive, commoditised and overcommunicated marketplace. Whether going for an interview or pitching for business, 'making a good first impression' is not enough to get us past first base. You need to be memorable, to stand out. When you have clarity and confidence in who you are, what you stand for, what value you bring and what difference you make, you will leave a lasting impression in the minds of prospective employers or customers. It's called personal branding.

The search for identity

At its core, personal branding is about identity; finding, defining and expressing who you are as a person. As children, our sense of identity is connected to others. Psychologists refer to 'identification', the unconscious process by which a child takes on the characteristics, attitudes, patterns of behaviour and emotions of their parents and other adult role models. During these early years, children also start forming their sense of self-esteem, primarily from their parents' view of them.

In adolescence, the search to develop a sense of individual identity becomes a confronting and evolving process. Adolescents question the values and moral standards they embraced as a child and start asking more self-reflective questions, such as 'who am I?' and 'where am I heading?'. They also start 'evaluating one's own behaviour as well as the behaviour of others…and feelings about one's own worth and competence'.[4]

In today's complex world, with limitless opportunities for study, travel and work, the search for identity may last for many years. In fact, many people spend a lifetime soul-searching, trying to understand and become comfortable with their personal identity.

In the world of work and business, the process of personal branding gives clarity and answers questions about self-identity, purpose, core beliefs and values and your worth. This clarity of identity is both empowering and powerful. When you have clarity about who you are and what you stand for, you are more confident to pursue your goals and seek opportunities. You also develop a deeper sense of being in control of your destiny and shaping your desired future.

We are in control of our personal brand identity. We are not, however, in control of our personal brand reputation because reputation is a perception that resides in the minds of others.

Personal brand versus reputation

Everyone has a reputation but not everyone has a personal brand. It is a critical distinction to understand.

Developing a personal brand is a decision by a person to distinguish themselves from others in the workplace or marketplace. It involves the intentional projection of an authentic identity with a distinctive style, voice, tonality and attitude. It encompasses a crafted personal narrative, value proposition and profile building activities. And, for many, it includes the visual elements of their personal brand identity, such as a logo, colours, symbols and shapes.

Not everyone has a personal brand because not everyone undertakes this deliberate and strategic process of defining, expressing and leveraging their authentic self-identity for the purpose of expanding their influence, elevating their worth or positioning themselves more favourably against 'competitor' alternatives.

However, everyone has a personal reputation. From the first impressions you make to the way you communicate and the actions you take, people are always forming opinions and assumptions about you based on their direct or indirect experience with you. Because reputation is perception, it can be different from person to person. So, unless you take control of your personal brand, your personal reputation is likely to be inconsistent among your colleagues or in your industry.

The rise of the internet and the global marketplace have firmly ushered in the era of the reputation economy. A generation or more ago, people formed an opinion about you from their direct experience with you in the workplace or what they heard others say about you. Nowadays, with the expansive online footprints individuals can create, people form opinions about you based on what they see and experience of you across all mediums – online, in person, in print or via electronic media.

The internet has also changed the way we make decisions. It is now standard practice to check the LinkedIn profile of a job candidate as part of the recruitment process or before having a coffee with a new business acquaintance. Through this scrutiny, we are making assumptions and forming biases based on what individuals say and how they behave online. We are checking out posts, blogs, videos, images and connections. And we are doing this 24/7.

These online experiences, together with face-to-face and other offline interactions, form pieces of a perceptual jigsaw puzzle. Anything you say and do on any medium can influence a person's perception about you, and what they say about you to others.

So, if you want to shape a desired reputation, take control of your personal brand today.

Super powers of personal branding

A strong, authentic and well-managed personal brand benefits you in myriad ways.

Purpose and meaning

Connecting with your purpose through your work or business is one of the most significant epiphanies you'll have in your life. The process of exploring your identity through the personal branding process is one of deep self-reflection which leads to a high level of self-awareness, clarity of purpose, vision and values.

When you wake every day and feel connected to a cause that inspires you, you will derive a strong sense of professional satisfaction and deep meaning from your work. The motivational force that clarity of purpose gives you has an extraordinary ripple effect beyond the service you deliver. It helps you think bigger picture and understand that your work makes the world a better place in some way.

Becoming clear on your purpose by defining your personal brand is one of the most powerful reputation-defining decisions you will make; you will unleash your Inner Brilliance in pursuit of your goals and, ultimately, a worthy legacy.

Clarity and confidence

There's a sense of positive energy that's contagious when you're in the company of someone who is genuinely confident in their own skin and clear about who they are, what they stand for, how they make a difference and where they're heading. This is what the process of personal branding gives you. From the articulation of purpose, vision and values to the expression of self-worth and definition of professional value, personal branding gives clarity to make decisions and confidence to act.

While there are many definitions of confidence, in their pursuit of the 'confidence code', studying the research, speaking with world experts and interviewing women leaders in politics, sports, the military and the arts, Katty Kay and Claire Shipman determined that 'Confidence is the stuff that turns thoughts into actions'[5].

While they found that confidence is part hardwired into your DNA, the brain can also rewire itself throughout life to cultivate confidence. Not by thinking positive thoughts day long or faking it till you make it but by embracing mindfulness, rituals and habits; by dropping confidence killers, such as people-pleasing and perfectionism; and by taking more risks, being action-oriented and failing fast.

You may already be confident at some things but not at others. People are generally more confident at activities they're competent at and unconfident at things they don't do very often or things they're fearful of. For instance, I'm confident at writing but unconfident at making videos, so my personal brand content is predominantly the written word. I know, however, that if I reframe my thinking about making videos, make it a habit every day to create a video on my phone, over time I'll build my 'video-making muscle' and become more confident.

Plasticity, Kay and Shipman conclude, 'is the cornerstone of the idea that confidence is a choice we can all make'[6]. Taking charge of your personal brand rather than leaving it to chance is also a choice. The process of self-discovery that occurs through the personal branding process will give you clarity and confidence to pursue your goals and dreams and achieve the extraordinary.

With this clarity comes confidence and certainty about your self-worth. When you truly believe you are good enough and value your professional self-worth, you will have the clarity, confidence and certainty to determine a price that reflects that value, to pitch for that amazing project, to grasp opportunities as they arise, and to attract clients and employers who also value your worth.

Standing apart

Personal brands stand out; others blend into a sea of sameness. I remember walking into the reception area of my new office building in 2016 and counting eight accounting firms listed on the business directory board. Assuming they're all great at what they do, how would I know which one to choose if I'm in the market for a new accountant? The answer is I wouldn't know unless they had a differentiated brand.

It's the same for people. In many service industries there's no shortage of consultants and coaches from whom to choose. But all things being equal, the professional who is clear about what they stand for, confident in their value and certain of their results, will stand out and have a competitive edge.

Reputational advantage

When you have a strong personal brand, your reputation precedes you. Because personal branding is an intentional strategy to build reputation, you can drive a more unified perception of who you are by amplifying your good character, capability and credibility, and increasing your exposure in all public domains.

In the digital and globally-connected marketplace of the 21st century, reputation is your most valuable intangible asset and critical to your professional success. Reputation doesn't sit at the bottom of the profit and loss statement but it absolutely affects the financial bottom line, for individuals and businesses. It's not surprising then that brand-savvy mega-entrepreneurs Richard Branson and Gary Vaynerchuk attribute reputation to their success. On Virgin, Richard Branson says 'The defining factor that has kept us in business, and growing, for more than 50 years has been the strength and reputation of the brand'[7]. Vaynerchuk says when it comes to personal branding 'reputation is the ultimate currency'[8].

What's your reputation worth? When I ask this question of my clients, without exception they say 'it's priceless!'. People are generally reluctant to put a dollar figure on their reputation because it is invaluable when it comes to building a successful career or business.

And while reputation is intangible, it has demonstrable tangible return on investment. For instance, research shows that organisations with a strong and positive reputation:

- attract, recruit and retain the best talent
- are perceived as providing more value so can charge higher prices
- have greater customer loyalty
- have greater influence when it comes to advocacy and negotiating
- are more likely to receive the benefit of the doubt from stakeholders in times of crisis.

On the flip side, having a poor reputation has tangible costs, such as reduced employee productivity and morale, higher employee turnover, lost sales, to name a few.

What holds true for organisations also applies to personal brands. When you have carved a solid reputation, you're more of a known quantity and, therefore, more likely to be perceived as a 'safer bet'.

Having a great personal reputation also has a halo effect; it reflects positively on your business. Research shows a strong correlation between the personal reputation of CEOs and that of their brands, particularly in founder-led businesses. This relationship is reciprocal. Personal reputational issues of a CEO can affect the reputation of the company's brands and vice versa; a damaged company brand can negatively impact the CEO's personal reputation.

A global study of more than 1,750 executives by Weber Shandwick and KRC Research found that 45% of a company's corporate reputation and 44% of its market value are attributable to its CEO's reputation. Furthermore, a positive CEO reputation is seen as integral in attracting and retaining employees.[9]

If you're an employee, particularly if you have career aspirations, having a strong personal brand is highly valuable. With a CareerBuilder survey[10] finding that 70 per cent of employers use social media to screen candidates during the hiring process, personal branding is an important career-building technique.

Authority positioning

An outcome of building a strong personal brand is becoming more well-known within your organisation, industry and networks. Another outcome is having the value of your ideas, advice and skills recognised.

When you deliver high value to customers, you're more able to charge premium pricing, especially if you have specialist expertise or a signature methodology unique to you.

In a highly competitive and commoditised marketplace, a signature methodology distinguishes you from others because it's what makes you different. Your signature methodology – whether it's a process, framework, system, technique, model or strategy, or a technology, game or piece of equipment, or other approach - should be part of your brand positioning and used as a key plank in your promotional strategy. It's why people will choose you over a competitor.

In a reputation economy, a strong personal brand accelerates the 'know, like, trust' process. Trust is the ultimate currency of business and workplace relationships and essential for building a great reputation. People want to hire, and do business with, people they trust or, at least, feel they can trust.

While trust is built over time, a strong personal brand can nurture a sense of trust in the absence of an established relationship. This is because when you cultivate a strong personal brand that consistently makes clear your unique character, qualities and capability, you cumulatively build a sense of familiarity, dependability and credibility in people's minds. Being known, liked and trusted in any industry or workplace is incredibly powerful positioning from which to scale a business or move up the corporate ladder.

Having a strong personal brand enhances your ability to leverage partnerships. A strong personal brand can make you more attractive to potential strategic partners when there is an opportunity to enhance each other's service offering for mutual financial benefit. I have been, and still am, involved in several long-term strategic partnerships where we refer clients to each other, provide testimonials, make introductions and bring many more benefits.

PART 2

MYTHS, TELLTALES AND LEGENDS

> 'One's philosophy is not best expressed in words; it is expressed in the choices one makes. In the long run, we shape our lives, and we shape ourselves. The process never ends until we die. And the choices we make are ultimately our own responsibility.'
>
> Eleanor Roosevelt, American political figure, diplomat and human rights activist

People can be apprehensive about personal branding for many reasons. This part busts some of the myths around personal branding, highlights signs that indicate you need personal branding, tells some legendary stories of personal brand lessons and unveils the one legendary lesson that unleashes Inner Brilliance.

Myths that keep your Inner Brilliance hidden

Sometimes, a person's perception of what personal branding is can hold them back from building their own personal brand. Here are seven personal brand myths that may be holding you back. And, like all myths, it's so much fun busting them!

Myth 1 – Building a personal brand is being fake

Your personal brand is not about being someone you're not. Quite the opposite, a personal brand simply amplifies who you are but in a more intentional, aligned and consistent way. A personal brand should be grounded, highlighting your unique attributes, values, strengths and zone of genius that set you apart.

If you cultivate a personal brand that's not true to who you are, it will become exhausting to keep up the charade. In fact, building a strong personal brand that is true to who you are can be liberating because you are giving yourself permission to be unashamedly and unapologetically you!

Myth 2 – A personal brand is only for high profile people

Personal branding is not about being famous; but it is about standing out. If you want to position yourself as an authority in your field or have career ambitions, you need to stand out. This is the entire point of personal branding. It is about becoming more distinguishable from the competition, more well-known in your field and more connected with others. And it can lead to you being tapped on the shoulder for more senior positions, being referred to potential new clients and generally being more in the spotlight.

The degree to which you position yourself as a person of influence through personal branding is an individual decision. You don't have to become super well-known or influential if you don't want to; you may wish to use the personal branding process to simply gain more clarity about your purpose, values and value proposition, for example. Having this clarity, however, will in itself make you more distinguishable from others as you are able to convey more eloquently your worth and what you stand for.

Myth 3 – Personal branding is only for extroverts

Personal branding is not based on, or for, certain personality types or traits. It's for any person in any industry and for many different reasons. You may need to channel your inner extrovert if putting yourself out there doesn't come second nature to you. However, by taking small steps you will become more comfortable over time.

Myth 4 – I don't need personal branding because people already know me

People may know you but do they perceive you the way you'd like to be perceived? If you've been under the radar for a long time, chances are, people may perceive you in different ways. In a competitive and commoditised marketplace, it makes sense to build a strong and consistent personal brand by design, rather than creating a weak and fragmented one by default. Personal branding reduces the risk that your reputation will be left to chance.

Do the right people know you? While you may be well-known among your immediate work colleagues, how well known are you within your industry, business networks or decision-makers within your target audiences? A personal brand means clearly identifying your target audiences, defining the problem you help them solve and articulating how you specifically do this, differently to others in your field. So, the goal is not just to be well-known but to be known by the right people for the right reasons.

Myth 5 - Personal branding is too much effort

Personal branding doesn't require too much effort but it does require being consistent in the way you speak and act, and doing this in alignment with your beliefs and values. This is especially important in the public domain because everything you post online, every word you say in a meeting, how you act under pressure, the way you make people feel and every written piece of marketing collateral you distribute, is shaping other people's perceptions of you.

Over time, being consistent and aligned with your thoughts, words and actions, builds your personal brand credibility and trustworthiness.

Myth 6 – Personal branding means I must share everything about me

While personal branding requires you to clarify what you stand for and share your opinions, ideas and insights, it doesn't mean sharing every detail of your personal life. You get to draw the line about what you share in the public domain – a good rule of thumb is using gut feel to understand whether sharing something publicly is within your comfort zone or makes you feel slightly nervous.

It's important to remember, however, with our expansive digital footprints available to view 24/7, the lines between our personal and professional lives are blurring.

No-one is perfect and people will expect a level of transparency and vulnerability so they get to know the real you. In fact, sharing your flaws and failings, and lessons learned, endears you even more to your followers because they get to see elements of their own imperfect life in you.

Myth 7 – Personal branding is a fast-track to success

Building a strong personal brand and desired reputation doesn't happen overnight. It takes strategy, combined with a plan of action and a way of managing the process. This process must be underpinned by strong commitment and consistency over time.

The good news is that as soon as you start to define and develop your personal brand, then think, speak, act and dress in accordance with it, you immediately take positive steps towards your professional goals and will begin to see benefits in the way you present yourself and make decisions.

> ***Activity – identifying your myths and barriers***
>
> What myths or barriers are currently holding you back from building your personal brand?
>
> _____
>
> _____
>
> _____
>
> _____
>
> _____
>
> _____
>
> _____
>
> _____
>
> _____
>
> _____

Telltale signs you need a personal brand

The following seven telltale signs can indicate that you need to build a strong personal brand or risk blending in with the pack. See if any resonate with you.

Telltale Sign 1 – You undervalue your self-worth

How highly you value your professional self-worth has a direct bearing on the results you will achieve in career and business. A common mindset I see with many talented professionals is undervaluing themselves and the service they deliver.

Self-doubt about professional capability or business acumen often leads people to question whether they are 'good enough'.

For example, 'Am I good enough to …

- pitch for this amazing job/project?
- charge a higher price for my service?
- run a public workshop?
- deliver a keynote presentation at a conference?
- publish an article on LinkedIn?
- do a media interview with the local journalist?

Negative thinking and associated self-talk keeps people stuck in a mindset of inaction and can inhibit professional growth and undermine business progress.

For instance, if you have low professional self-worth, you are more likely to:

- devalue the service you offer and charge below the market rate
- only sell your time rather than pricing your services based on the unique value you deliver in solving a high-value problem
- not take advantage of opportunities, preferring to stay in your comfort zone
- stay a commoditised 'vanilla' brand rather than stand out from competitors.

Ultimately, the success you truly desire will remain elusive until you change your mindset around your professional self-worth. The process of personal branding will help improve your self-image and give you more confidence to put yourself out there.

Telltale Sign 2 – Your words and actions don't align with your values

Sometimes in life, business and work, we say and do things that do not align with our true selves. We may do this to fit in, to get along, to people please, to stay under the radar, to not rock the boat, to puff ourselves up, to bring ourselves down, among others. However, speaking and acting out of alignment with our true values and beliefs feels uncomfortable and is a disservice to self.

People with a strong personal brand are grounded in reality. They have an unwavering and unapologetic way of being true to themselves by thinking, speaking and acting in alignment with their beliefs and values. This powers up their confidence, presence and influence in the marketplace, workplace and in the boardroom.

Telltale Sign 3 – You're not clear on your 'why'

You know what you do and how you do it, but you may not be clear on why you do it. In today's purpose-driven world, people want to connect with brands that stand for more than just profits. Getting clear on your purpose – your 'why' – is essential to engage hearts and minds.

When businesses embrace a higher purpose beyond making money, they can make a stronger emotional connection with their target audiences, including employees, who can link their work to an inspiring end cause. A global survey of business executives conducted by Harvard Business Review Analytic Services and EY Beacon Institute[11], found that companies that clearly identified their purpose as 'an aspirational reason for being which inspires and provides a call to action for an organisation and its partners and stakeholders, and provides benefit to local and global society' reported that their customers were more loyal and employees more engaged.

It's also important for personal brands to be crystal clear on their why so each day they can connect with a driving force that gives them energy, purpose and meaning, and become a beacon for those they wish to connect with or influence.

Telltale Sign 4 – You're too 'vanilla'

Do you feel that in business or at work you're just blending in with the crowd and not being noticed by those whose attention you wish to attract? Having a strong personal brand makes you more distinguishable so you stand out from the rest. International award-winning television and film producer, and creator of some of the most watched reality shows, including *Big Brother*, *The X Factor* and *Dancing with the Stars*, Maz Farrelly, is an expert in standing out. One of her gold nuggets when it comes to standing out is, 'It is not my job to be interested – it is your job to be interesting!'[12].

People pay more attention to that which is interesting. Your you-niqueness automatically makes you interesting. That being a fact, the personal branding process will enhance your 'interestingness' by crafting your vision, values and value proposition into an inspiring personal narrative that reflects your unique style, attitude and voice.

Telltale Sign 5 – People don't know what you do

If you're having trouble attracting your ideal client or communicating your worth to your employer, it could be because people don't understand or are confused about the problem you solve or the value you deliver.

A simple, clear message about what you do and the value you provide improves connection with your target audience. This rings true whether you're at a barbecue or making an important sales pitch. Being clear in your message – verbally and in writing – makes it easier for others to engage with you, buy from you and, ultimately, become an advocate for you.

Telltale Sign 6 – You have no visibility

You know you're great at what you do but it's hard to climb the corporate ladder or run a successful business if no-one else knows you exist. To be considered for that senior position or ideal client contract, you first need to be known. For workers, this could mean becoming a known quantity by the organisational executive or human resources team. For businesspeople, this could mean turning up in search results or building a profile in the local community.

One of the key advantages of having a strong personal brand is you become more visible within your workplace or industry. This doesn't happen just because you have gained clarity on your personal brand vision and values; you must be intentional with your thoughts, words and actions. This might mean sharing your thoughts and ideas on social media, taking on committee positions, attending functions and events, expanding your industry networks, volunteering or writing articles for newsletters, for example.

Becoming more visible means being intentional about building your digital footprint so that when you come up in search results, your personal brand is consistent across platforms. There are many things you can do to become more found on the internet, such as ensuring your website, LinkedIn profile and other online presences are search engine optimised, using the right key words, being listed on the right business directories and using image tags.

Telltale Sign 7 – People's perception of you varies

People build trust with other people when they have a sense of familiarity and understanding. If you're not showing up, online or in person, with regularity and consistency, then people may describe you in different ways or be confused about what you stand for. This lack of familiarity or confusion can be a blockage for some people to reach out to you when it comes to connecting on social media or discussing work or business opportunities, simply because they are unsure if you are the right person or a good fit.

Personal branding helps you shape a more unified perception of who you are and leverage this to enhance your credibility, marketability and trustworthiness. This increases the likelihood that others will reach out to you based on a belief, opinion or assumption that you are likely to be a good match.

> ### Activity – identifying your telltale signs
>
> What signs are telling you that a strong personal brand will benefit your career or business?
>
> _____
>
> _____
>
> _____
>
> _____
>
> _____

Legendary personal brand lessons

If you're the face of your business, you are the business, so building a good name is imperative in a marketplace where word-of-mouth referrals hold strong sway. It's the same in the workplace; as you build your personal brand, your name is the reason you'll get tapped on the shoulder and asked to apply for jobs even when you are not looking.

What's in a name?

Tina Turner – 'Simply the Best' name

When legendary singer, songwriter and entertainer Tina Turner left Ike Turner following years of abuse, the only thing she wanted was her name – Tina Turner. While no doubt she could have claimed material possessions from her successful stage career as half of the Ike and Tina Turner duo, it was the name the mattered most. For it was the Tina Turner stage name – her personal brand – that was already established and known, and from which she could rebuild her career and celebrity status as a solo artist. And this she did. When Tina passed away in May 2023, she had achieved legendary status and was known as the 'Queen of Rock'.

Julius Caesar – a pitiful ransom for nobility

The story goes that in 75BC, a band of pirates captured a young Roman nobleman named Julius Caesar who was on his way to study oratory at Rhodes. Understanding his position as a nobleman, Caesar didn't act like a person being held in captivity. He laughed at the pirates who were not aware of his status. When they told him they'd set his ransom at 20 talents, Caesar demanded they raise it to 50 talents, an amount more suitable of his position. After 38 days the ransom was paid and Caesar was set free. He returned at the head of a Roman fleet, found the pirates and had them killed.

Beyonce – Queen B by name and nature

In response to controversy about a perceived lip-synced performance of the American national anthem on the steps on the White House for President Obama's inauguration, Beyonce silenced her critics several days later by opening a press conference with a live rendition of the anthem. She asked all those at the conference to stand up while she belted out *The Star Spangled Banner*, then said, 'Any questions?' They don't call her Queen B for nothing.

Names add value but will only get you so far

Celebrity endorsements take advantage of the halo effect. Celebrities with strong personal brands (and great reputations) are often used to endorse products because companies know it increases brand awareness, anchors sentiment and boosts sales. Think George Clooney and Nespresso coffee, Michael Jordan and Nike footwear, Oprah and Weight Watchers.

But what happens when something goes wrong - when the celebrity does something bad or in poor taste in their personal or professional life? This can lead to a cutting of the ties between the celebrity and the product because of the halo effect; the poor choices and actions of the celebrity are perceived to also bring the endorsed product into disrepute. Golfer Tiger Woods, for example, lost endorsement contracts because of high-publicised infidelity; seven-time winner of the Tour de France Lance Armstrong lost endorsement contracts when evidence confirmed his use of banned substances; and British model Kate Moss lost luxury brand endorsements for reported drug use.

You may not have ambitions to be a celebrity, but their lessons are valid for anyone building a personal brand because your name can both open doors and close doors. That's why it's important to remember that your personal brand is considered in light of your reputation.

Having good capability and good communication are not enough, you must also have good character. Character is to reputation as reality is to perception. Character is who we really are; reputation is how we are perceived. Like a shadow, your reputation follows you wherever you go, shaped by the expression of your character through words and actions – in person, in print and online.

In my career I have seen many examples where the alleged/perceived misdemeanours of one person have impacted the reputation of an entire organisation. I have seen employees refuse to wear their nametags in public for fear of verbal abuse from the local community who may be frustrated, upset or angry with the organisation because of the alleged actions of one person. In these instances, the perceived lack of credibility of character impacted the reputation of the organisations they represented.

The one legendary lesson that unleashes Inner Brilliance

Mythographer Joseph Campbell's 'Hero's Journey', which describes a narrative in which a heroic protagonist sets out on a quest, faces trials and tribulations through multiple adventures, and returns home transformed, is a monomyth, 'a universal pattern that is the essence of, and common to, heroic tales in every culture'.[13]

The Hero's Journey is a common framework used in many movies - think Luke in *Star Wars*, Dorothy in *The Wizard of Oz*, Neo in *The Matrix*, Clarke in *Superman*, Harry in *Harry Potter and the Philosopher's Stone*, Rocky in the *Rocky* movies, Frodo in *Lord of the Rings*, Daniel in *The Karate Kid* and even Simba in *The Lion King*.

The secret behind all these movies is that the hero becomes a better version of themselves not because of the influence of some external force but because of discovering what they needed was always inside of themselves.

In the *Wizard of Oz*, the Good Witch Glinda explains to Dorothy that 'You've always had the power to go back to Kansas' but that she didn't tell her that earlier 'because she wouldn't have believed me. She had to learn it for herself'.

In Star Wars, Obi-Wan Kenobi says to Luke Skywalker 'Use the Force, Luke' to inspire him to summon his innate powerful energy force to achieve his true destiny as a Jedi Knight and challenge the dark forces.

This inner knowing, inner energy, inner mojo, is the secret of personal branding, if there is a secret, and the core message of this book. Personal branding is fundamentally about bringing forth all your inner passions, personality, character, strengths, talents, skills, knowledge and creative genius – your Inner Brilliance – to be the best version of yourself.

Here are some examples of modern day 'heroes' who have embraced their Inner Brilliance and use it to their professional advantage as well as for the greater good.

- Australian sports champion Ash Barty embraced her Inner Brilliance for playing tennis, her innate humility and vulnerability, and her Aboriginal heritage to become a First Nations Tennis Ambassador and role model to young people throughout the world.
- Iconic American talk show host Oprah Winfrey embraced her Inner Brilliance for empathy and compassion to be an inspirational role model and help others get through difficult times.

Your Inner Brilliance Is Your Superpower!

PART 3

GOING FROM ZERO TO HERO

'You must take personal responsibility. You cannot change the circumstances, the seasons or the wind, but you can change yourself. That is something you have charge of.'
Jim Rohn, American entrepreneur, author and motivational speaker

What unleashes Inner Brilliance?

When passion, purpose and vision converge, a potent energy force unleashes your Inner Brilliance – your creative genius – that results in a highly valuable outcome.

Inner Brilliance is highly individual and manifests in many ways, such as:

- the expression of an idea
- the performance of a talent or skill
- the application of specialist subject matter from theory to practice
- a creative work
- development of a strategy
- the solving of a complex problem
- the delivery of a service.

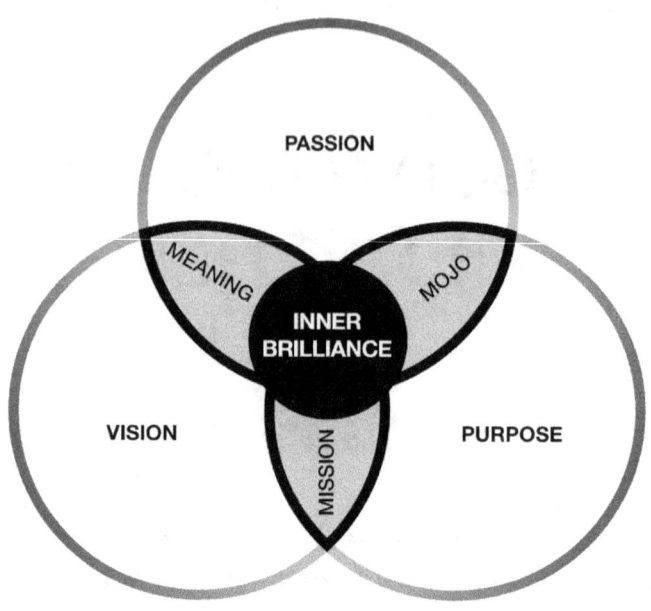

Inner Brilliance Model™ ©Ros Weadman

Passions include activities that you love to do; that light you up and make you come alive. When you direct your passion into a purposeful goal or worthy cause that's meaningful to you, and you have a vivid vision about what outcome/success looks like, you will be highly motivated and bring forth all of your creative energy, talents, personality, intelligence, knowledge and skills (Inner Brilliance) to achieve that outcome.

For example, I'm passionate about education and empowering people with knowledge and skills so they can do more and be more. It's why I trained as a teacher many years ago, it's why I derive much satisfaction and fulfilment from my coaching, mentoring and training programs, and it's why my books always have a practical element so the theory can be translated easily into practice. My purposeful goal is to help people, businesses and organisations to effectively communicate their value and speak their legacy. My vision ties into this purpose, which is to create a community of visionary and purpose-driven brands that move humanity forward.

When you direct your passions into a worthy cause and have a vivid picture in your mind of the big picture difference it will make to others, you will wake every day with a deep knowing of why your work matters and through the application of your Inner Brilliance, you will leave an indelible mark on the world.

Your Inner Brilliance is the marketable value of your personal brand

Another way of considering your Inner Brilliance is your zone of genius; the area of work excellence that is of measurable value to your clients or organisation.

Because your Inner Brilliance is unique and highly valuable, it enables you to command premium pricing for your specialist problem-solving capability. You've most likely heard the story about the giant ship with a broken-down engine that no one could fix so the company hired a specialist engineer. After inspecting the engine carefully, the engineer pulled out a small hammer from his bag and tapped something gently. The engine then started. When the engineer gave the ship owner the invoice for $20,000 the owner was shocked, saying the engineer hardly did anything and demanding a detailed bill. The engineer said the breakdown of cost is simple, 'tap with a hammer: $2 and knowing where to knock and how much to knock: $19,998'.

Expressing your Inner Brilliance is good for you mentally and emotionally

The benefits of expressing your Inner Brilliance are many. For instance, when you're fully immersed in what you're doing with a feeling of energised focus on a project or activity that lights you up, you experience:

- **a state of focus and flow** – in positive psychology, this is known as a flow state, or 'being in the zone'. This state enables better performance, with less distraction and self-judgement and more motivation
- **mission and meaning** – your efforts are contributing to something that has special meaning to you
- **joy and fulfilment** – the release of mood-boosting chemicals such as dopamine and endorphins, which makes you feel good, like the 'runner's high' athletes strive to achieve.

Using the Inner Brilliance Personal Branding™ system you will clarify your passions, purpose and vision so you can unleash your personal brand Inner Brilliance in pursuit of your career aspirations.

Moving from invisible to influential

Building a personal brand and becoming more known for your Inner Brilliance is like removing a cloak of invisibility and the world seeing you in all your magnificence. Not only will you be more noticed, but your level of influence will also expand because people will be interested in your perspective and your known expertise.

When it comes to building a strong personal brand and being considered in the top echelon of your industry, people usually sit on a spectrum from being invisible to being an industry VIP (very influential person). The below table shows the indicative Inner Brilliance Personal Branding™ journey, from being invisible and totally under the radar, to becoming an Industry VIP and fully focused on leaving your mark on the world.

PERSONAL BRAND INFLUENCE SPECTRUM

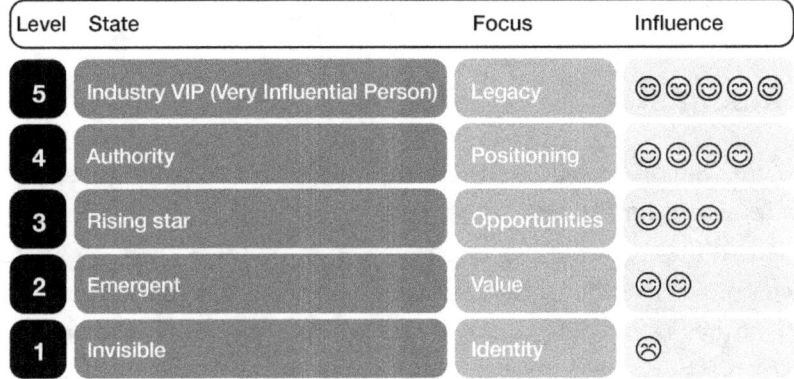

Inner Brilliance Personal Brand Influence Spectrum ©Ros Weadman

Where are you on the Inner Brilliance Personal Brand Influence Spectrum?

1. Invisible

You are considered to be a '**quiet achiever**'. Your strengths and expertise are recognised by those you work closest with but you fly under the radar outside of the workplace and within your industry. This positioning may have suited you up until now, but as time goes on you notice that staying out of the limelight isn't doing you any favours as opportunities are passing you by. You start to question who you are and what you are capable of. You focus on your **identity**.

2. Emergent

You are starting to be recognised as '**someone to watch**' in your industry/workplace and to attract new business or roles based on your growing knowledge and experience. You're also recognised for your commitment to achieving results for your organisation or clients. You may be becoming more ambitious in your career or business or realise that cultivating a personal brand is going to set you apart from the competition. You start to question what you want to achieve and how you might achieve it. You focus on your **value**.

3. Rising star

You are gaining a reputation as a '**top performer**' in your industry/workplace and attracting higher paying clients or leadership roles based on the results you are achieving and the relationships you are building. You may be thinking of taking on volunteer roles on boards, committees or project groups to broaden your professional network, build your leadership skills and become more well-known within your industry. You start to know that you are made for more, that your character and competencies will take you places. You focus on **opportunities**.

4. Authority

You are a recognised '**subject matter expert**' within your industry, are highly paid, and have a loyal and growing client base. You are respected among peers and sought after for advice. You are now specialised in your field, which differentiates you from others, and valued by the type of organisations or market segment that you have chosen to serve. You question what is needed to lead your field in the years ahead. You focus on **positioning**.

5. Industry VIP (Very Influential Person)

You are recognised as a '**master**' in your field and a leader in your industry. You have a full book of clients who pay a premium price and top clients seek you out. Your opinion holds sway within your industry. Your ideas and insights contribute to the advancement of thinking within your industry. You keep questioning everything because you know that even being masterful at something doesn't mean you know everything. You focus on leaving a **legacy**.

Your personal brand comes to life the moment you decide it matters. You are responsible for how you show up in the world – what you think, say and do – even when no-one else is in the room. So, from right now, you can start being your personal brand and let a more intentional, aligned, consistent and authentic version of you shape the reputation you desire.

Activity – your influence now and in the future

Where are you now on the personal brand influence spectrum?

_____

_____

_____

Where do you want to be in one/two/five/ten years' time? Why?

_____

_____

_____

In which areas do you want to be more influential in your career/business:

- with clients/my team?
- within my industry?
- within my workplace?
- in meetings?
- public speaking?
- sales conversations?
- in the media?
- other?

_____

_____

_____

Unleashing the force within you

In *Star Wars*, The Force was an energy field that bound the galaxy together. The 'light' side of The Force is what gave a Jedi his/her power for the good of the galaxy; the 'dark' side of The Force was defined by anger, fear, aggression and lust for power. Through his mentor Obi-Wan Kenobi, Luke, a Jedi pilot in the making, learned how to conjure The Force from within. This gave him a strong sense of identity, sharpened his intuition, emboldened his courage and conjured his lightsabre in the fight scenes against nemesis Darth Vader. Like Luke, your Inner Brilliance is the force within you and you must learn how to tap into it to let it shine and drive you energetically to achieve great things.

Building a strong authentic personal brand doesn't happen in a vacuum. However, with intention, alignment, consistency and authenticity, you can leverage your personal brand in a most powerful way.

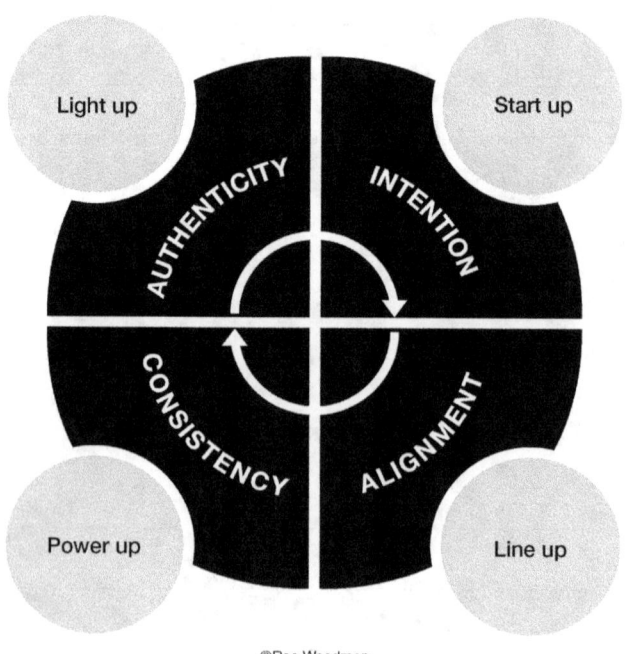

©Ros Weadman

Intention

It all starts with intention - a desire to shift, an attitude to evolve and a commitment to take action to become a personal brand with influence and worth.

Intention sets in train decisions to gain clarity on your purpose, your beliefs and values, your message, your specialist value, your leadership style, your presence. In essence, how you intend to show up to the outside world.

At the heart of this intention is a shift to adopting a personal brand mindset and all that goes with it, including the responsibility and accountability for what you think, say and do.

Brand is an inside job of which reputation is an external manifestation. Understanding that the principle of cause and effect applies to brand and reputation is an empowering concept for professionals to embrace.

Your brand is 100 per cent within your control – from the values you uphold to the image you project, the messages you convey, the actions you take, the body language you use, the clothes you wear – putting you in the driver's seat of shaping how you want to be perceived.

If you are intentional in all these areas, you'll build a strong personal brand and forge a desired reputation in the minds of those who matter to you and/or those whom you want to influence.

Alignment

People with a strong personal brand think, speak and act in alignment with their beliefs and values. This alignment gives them confidence, presence and influence.

Think of sports stars, such as Ash Barty and Roger Federer, or political leaders, such as former New Zealand prime minister Jacinda Ardern or former Finland prime minister Sanna Marin.

Although holding the country's most senior position, Sanna Marin stood firm on her belief to unapologetically express her youth, after a leaked video showed her dancing and singing with friends at a private function.

Similarly, Jacinda Ardern's belief in a compassionate and open communication style of leadership, rejecting the premise that prime ministers must be aggressive and masculine, became a beacon of what effective and modern political leadership looks like.

Consistency

Consistency builds visibility, trust and momentum. If you're consistent with your brand presence, online and in person, you're more likely to build a cohesive brand reputation because people gain a more unified understanding of who you are and what you're about.

Consistency of brand presence also fosters trust with people because when you consistently make clear your unique character, qualities and capability, you cumulatively build a sense of familiarity, dependability and credibility in people's minds. Over time, consistency builds your public profile as your thoughts and ideas come more under the spotlight, with your message lighting up more of those around you.

Authenticity

What makes us individually different from each other is the secret sauce or X-factor of a personal brand. While intention, alignment and consistency are universal attributes or habits that all people can embrace, authenticity is unique to everyone. No-one thinks, speaks or does things like you. It's your you-niqueness that ultimately sets you apart.

In other words, your personal brand is the authentic you. While you may think authenticity is a given when it comes to personal branding, unfortunately that's not always the case. In the world of people branding, the persona that someone projects may not always be their authentic self. Actors, for example, may project an image befitting of the character roles they play in the movies, but this may not be consistent with who they are in everyday life.

PART 4

THE INNER BRILLIANCE PERSONAL BRANDING™ SYSTEM

Inner Brilliance Personal Branding System™ ©Ros Weadman

This section provides the practical blueprint to develop a strong personal brand. It explores in depth each of the four key outcomes of the Inner Brilliance Personal Branding™ system – **purpose**, **positioning**, **profile** and **profitability** – and gives you activities and practical tools for each of the eight steps.

The system summarised

The Inner Brilliance Personal Branding™ system is designed to help you achieve four key outcomes:

1. Clarity of personal brand **purpose**
2. Establishment of personal brand **positioning**
3. Building a personal brand **profile**
4. Optimising personal brand **profitability**

Outcome 1: Purpose

The purpose dimension of the system taps into the fire within that ignites your motivations and desires **(passion)**, and gains clarity on the purpose that drives you to derive meaning through your work and make your mark on the world by striving towards a compelling future **(vision)**.

Step 1: Verve – Spark your passion

Your verve is your vibe; it's the raw energy that fuels your passions and drives your positive attitude to life. When you do things you're passionate about, you're at your happiest. The endorphins flow through your body, your vibration elevates and you derive a sense of purpose and wellbeing. Your positive vibe not only energises you, but the emotional contagion also uplifts others.

Step 2: Vision – Envision your legacy

Your vision is what the world looks like because you are delivering on your passion and purpose. It is a north star for your strategic direction and helps people understand what you stand for. Your vision also provides an anchor when times get tough - it gets you out of bed each day in pursuit of the positive difference you seek to make.

Outcome 2: Positioning

The positioning dimension of the system helps to differentiate you from others based on the high standards you uphold **(values)** and the solution you deliver through your specialist problem-solving intelligence and skillset **(value)**. Through effective positioning, your personal brand will capture the interest of your target audience and elevate your standing within your industry.

Step 3: Values – Uphold your standards

Values are fundamental to your personal brand; they guide your thinking, decision-making, language and behaviour. Also known as principles, values dictate what you deem as important and strive to always uphold in your professional and personal life.

Step 4: Value – Differentiate your expertise

Your value is in how you well you solve a problem people are willing to pay for. Through your work you are a catalyst of change. You have expertise that helps take your client, team or organisation from where they are now to where they want to be. Your target market highly values, and will pay handsomely, for the benefits derived from delivering your value to them.

Outcome 3: Profile

The profile dimension of the system is about communicating your personality **(voice)** and building your presence **(visibility)** in the marketplace and industry. Through profile building, you extend your reach across networks and become more influential in your industry.

Step 5: Voice – Communicate your personality

Everyone communicates, but only personal brands are heard. Your personal brand has a story that cuts through the white noise with a bold, brilliant message. Delivered in a language and tonality that reflects your personal style and attitude, your message will resonate deeply and strongly.

Step 6: Visibility – Elevate your presence

Your visibility is your brilliant presence in the marketplace. A consistent and aligned public profile across all digital channels and in-person touchpoints accelerates the 'know, like, trust' process with others. A content ecosystem that uses the right mediums to convey your message to the right audiences can build your profile by extending your reach and strengthening your brand positioning.

Outcome 4: Profitability

The profitability dimension of the system is about commercialising your thought leadership to grow your business or advance your career with steady momentum **(velocity)** and putting in place systems and protections to shore up a more sustainable future **(viability)**.

Step 7: Velocity – Accelerate your momentum

Your packaged products are the signature services, programs and events you deliver. Packaging your intellectual property into a product ecosystem, that includes a variety of delivery modes and meets different customer needs, will scale your business exponentially.

Step 8: Viability – Secure your success

As your authority positioning builds in the marketplace and within your industry, maintaining a positive personal brand mindset over time and managing your personal brand are essential for sustainable success.

Purpose – Ignite your personal brand

Tap into the DNA that makes you tick; the energy that fires your ambitions; the purpose that drives you to live a meaningful life and make your mark on the world.

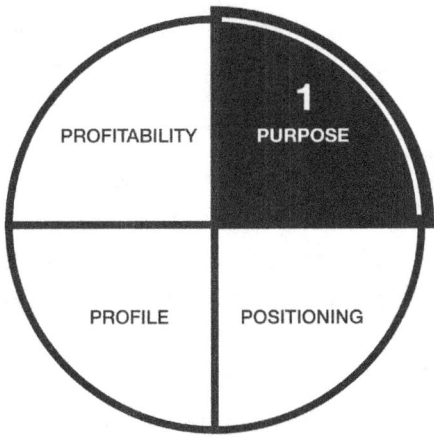

Step 1: Verve – Spark your passion

> *'Passion is an affair of the heart, meaning is an affair of the mind and purpose is an affair of the soul.'*
> Ros Weadman, strategic communications expert

Choosing why, what, how and for whom you contribute your individual passion, knowledge, skills, talents, energy, time and efforts is an important decision for everyone. When your work ignites the fire within, awakens a sense of purpose and aligns with your highest values, you not only experience deep personal fulfilment, but the fruits of your labour create positive ripples well beyond the workplace.

Passion

What lights you up?

When you do things you're passionate about, you become 'more alive' physically, mentally and emotionally. Your energy vibration uplifts, your face lights up and you become super focused on the activity at hand spurred by the rush of dopamine and endorphins flowing palpably through your body.

Sure, everyone has good and bad days at work, but when you're passionate about the cause of the organisation, your passion will pull you through. In his book *Brainfluence*, Roger Dooley says passion is palpable and can be felt by customers so it pays to look beyond resumes and facts when recruiting staff to represent your brand. 'Your customers can sense the passion of your people, even if they don't process it. The body language, the speech patterns and other cues will give your customers the confidence that the person they are dealing with truly believes in your product.'[14]

Passion is a precursor to purpose; knowing what drives you energetically helps you identify projects and workplaces more likely to fulfil you. For instance, a PWC 2016 study about purpose in the workplace found that Millennials (born between 1980 and 1995) are 5.3 times more likely to stay with an employer when they have a strong connection to their employer's purpose.[15]

In his iconic research on the attributes of the world's greatest companies, Jim Collins found the essential strategic difference between the good-to-great companies and the comparison companies was that the former had a deep understanding and were able to execute on three key dimensions of what became known as the Hedgehog Concept[16]:

- What you are deeply passionate about
- What you can be the best in the world at
- What drives your economic engine

Collins says that passion, as a key part of an organisation's strategic framework, can't be manufactured; you can only discover what ignites your passion and the passions of others: 'The good-to-great companies did not say, 'Okay, folks, let's get passionate about we do'. Sensibly, they went the other way entirely: We should only do those things that we can get passionate about.'[17]

So, the question is, how do you find something you can get passionate about?

Search for meaning

Passion is an affair of the heart and needs a cause to which it can engage the mind to find meaning. Victor Frankl's iconic 1946 literary work, *Man's Search for Meaning*, which chronicles his horrifying experiences as a prisoner in Nazi concentration camps, along with his psychotherapeutic approach to survive, highlights the importance of finding meaning in your life.

Frankel believed that people are motivated by a 'will to meaning'[18], which equates to an inner desire to find meaning in life. Frankel's philosophy is a useful paradigm for personal brands because when you consider we can spend about a third of our life at work, it makes sense to be able to direct our natural passions towards a role, project or cause to which we can contribute our skills and talents and, in return, experience fulfilment, satisfaction and joy derived from a sense of meaning.

Your passion comes from deep within you. Discovering what you're passionate about or what you can get passionate about through your work requires asking some questions about the kinds of things that motivate you and give you the most pride, satisfaction and meaning at work. The below questions are a good starting point.

Discovering your passion

- At what times in your life did you love what you were doing while you were doing it?
    - were you being compassionate towards others?
    - were you empowering others?
    - were you leading others?
    - were you using your creative talents?
    - were you travelling?
- What kind of work inspires you?
    - educating others?
    - working to improve the health and wellbeing of others?
    - helping those with disability to live a life of joy and meaning?
    - working in research to find a cure for a particular illness?
    - helping improve the state of the natural environment?
    - working in the not-for profit sector to help people who are disadvantaged?
    - working to improve the wellbeing of animals?
- What kind of environment do you like working in?
    - the natural environment?
    - a place of education?
    - as part of a high-performing team?
    - on your own?
- What kinds of tasks and projects at work energise you?
    - working in research?
    - working on strategy?

- solving large, complex problems?
- working on large, complex projects?
- creative pursuits?

- What's important to your professional growth?
  - What new skills do you want to learn?
  - What topic areas are you most interested in?
  - What new knowledge do you want to acquire?
  - What opportunities exist to try new roles and positions?

Consider these hypothetical questions to tap into your passions and find a meaningful cause that you can pursue through your work or career:

- If you knew you had to retire one year from now, what kind of work would you do?
- At your retirement function, what aspect of your work/career will you be most proud of?
- If money, status or qualifications were no object, what kind of work/career would you pursue?

Being aware of your passion and connecting it to a cause is a pathway for personal brands to unleash their Inner Brilliance. When you know your passion, you will seek out jobs and careers that are more likely to bring you happiness and satisfaction, and you'll be inspired to do your best work. By so doing, you will inspire others to do the same.

Passion, a pathway to purpose

I believe that when you channel your passion into a meaningful cause in your work or career, you have landed on your personal brand purpose.

The word 'purpose' means the reason for which something is done, created or exists. It is often used synonymously with intention, goal, outcome, big idea, mission, expectation. Purpose is what we think about why we exist. In the aforementioned book *Good to Great*, Jim Collins says that passion can be focused on what the company stands for; that is, it's purpose.

As a personal brand, finding purpose from your passion is one of the most significant epiphanies you will have in your career. A declaration of purpose reveals what a personal brand believes in; the cause they have aligned themselves with. It defines why their work matters and helps those they work with understand why they do what they do.

It's not necessarily an easy or quick process to distil your personal brand purpose to just a few powerful words, but once you land on it, it's worth the investment of your time and consideration.

Let's consider some examples from the corporate world:

- Maker of durable outdoor clothing products that cause less harm to the environment, Patagonia, expresses its purpose as, 'We're in business to save our home planet'. This purpose underpinned its decision to establish the Patagonia Purpose Trust to protect its values and channel excess profits to the Holdfast Collective to fight the environmental crisis, protect nature and biodiversity, and support thriving communities.[19]
- Virgin puts purpose at the core of its identity - 'What makes us Virgin?' - with its declaration that 'For five decades, in five sectors and on five continents, our purpose is to change business for good'. The organisation's Chief Purpose and Vision Officer drives the alignment of purpose across the group's various brands.[20]
- CRM software developer Salesforce's co-CEO Marc Benioff says, 'The business of business is to make the world a better place'. This belief drives its core values of trust, customer success, innovation and equality of every human being.[21]

However, you don't have to be a big-name brand to have a great brand purpose. One of my favourite small businesses, L&D Picturesque Painting, a female-owned and operated painting business in Melbourne, is not only renowned for its punctual and precise painting prowess, but also for trailblazing a new path for women in trade industries by helping create a world where females are empowered, encouraged and confident to succeed. They've committed to 'leading by example and being positive role models for women in a traditionally male-dominated industry'.[22]

Know your 'why'

One way of clarifying your purpose is to find your 'why'. Renowned Ted Talker, visionary and author Simon Sinek's 'Start with Why'[23] mantra drives home how brand loyalty is built by emotionally connecting with your customers through the power of 'why'. His message is people don't buy *what* you do, they buy *why* you do it.

All businesses know what they do in terms of their product or service delivery and how they do it in terms of the process or methodology. But far fewer organisations know why they do what they do. Or, if they do know why, they may not know how to articulate this. So, from a marketing perspective, they focus on the what (product) and the how (features and benefits), which renders them commodity-based businesses in the eyes of consumers. It's the same with people. Everyone knows what their position description is and how they do their job but not everyone can articulate the why behind the what and the how of the tasks they perform daily.

Your 'why' is very often inspired by your passion in life – what lights you up – and your vision – the difference you seek to make in the world, or simply by considering the ripple effect on society of what you do every day in business for your clients.

The most powerful 'whys' are an expression of love

If your professional 'why' isn't an expression of love in some form, you may not have articulated your higher personal brand purpose.

I'm not talking about the romantic kind of love but a version of love that improves people's lives or the planet in some way and moves humanity forward.

Love can be expressed in different ways through your 'why', depending on the contribution and impact you make on people's lives through your work. For example:

- Self-acceptance
- Self-esteem
- Connection
- Community connectedness
- Confidence
- Belonging
- Peace of mind
- Optimism
- Autonomy
- Empowerment
- Hope
- Joy
- Fulfilment
- Health
- Wellbeing
- Healing
- Gratitude
- Forgiveness
- Freedom
- Resilience

To land on a 'why' that articulates a manifestation of love often requires asking the question, 'For what purpose?' several times.

For instance, a physiotherapist may articulate their 'why' as 'helping people with mobility challenges to rebuild their physical strength and reduce their pain'.

1. For what purpose? So they can move their bodies more freely and function better in their everyday lives.
2. For what purpose? So they can regain their independence and confidence.
3. For what purpose? So they can reconnect with and do things that bring them joy and lead a more fulfilling life.

The third statement is a higher-purpose 'why' statement because reconnection, joy and fulfilment are expressions of self-love.

Here's another example. A digital marketer may articulate their 'why' as 'helping small businesses get more customer leads through high-conversion websites'.

1. For what purpose? So they can sell more products and services.
2. For what purpose? So they can increase their profits.
3. For what purpose? So they can build a sustainable business doing work they love with customers who are a perfect match.

Again, the third statement is a higher purpose 'why' because it is connected to a manifestation of love.

Activity – find the 'why' in your work

Start by writing down why you do what you do, expressed as an outcome for your customer. Then ask, 'for what purpose?' at least three times until you land on a 'higher purpose why'.

- Why I do what I do for a living.

_____

_____

_____

_____

_____

- For what purpose?

_____

_____

_____

- For what purpose?

_____

_____

_____

- For what purpose?

_____

_____

_____

Step 2: Vision – Envision your legacy

> *'Your vision will become clear only when you can look into your own heart. Who looks outside, dreams; who looks inside, awakens.'*
> Carl Jung, Swiss psychiatrist and psychoanalyst

Your personal brand vision provides a North Star, giving you a clear direction in your professional life and in the difference you want to make in society that's connected to your passion and purpose. A compelling vision guides you when making strategic decisions about which opportunities to say yes and no to, what knowledge and skills to develop, and what experiences you want to have, so that you can stride towards this desired future.

A clear vision also provides personal brands with an anchor when times get tough. When things go off track because of life, when risks you took don't pan out, or when obstacles get in the way, a clear vision is like a lighthouse that helps you navigate rough seas and continue towards your destination.

Crafting a personal brand vision statement

In my work developing personal brand vision statements for business owners, organisational executives and community leaders, I've found that the most powerful vision statements have both an inward (self) and outward (others) focus.

With this twin focus, a personal brand vision statement answers the question, 'where am I heading in my career?'. And from a planetary perspective, it answers the question, 'what is the big picture outcome I want to make in the world through my work?'. The big picture difference is the legacy you leave as the result of your life's work.

It's how you make the world a better place because of your Inner Brilliance.

So, the Inner Brilliance personal brand vision framework guides you to answer two key questions:

1. What do you want to be known for?
2. What difference do you want to make?

When the answers to these questions are combined, the vision articulates what the personal brand wants to achieve for themselves professionally (inward focus) and what they want to achieve for the greater good (outward focus).

Professional vision

What do you want to be known for?

This question explores what you want to be known for in terms of your professional standing within your industry and what you want to be renowned for in terms of brand reputation. In other words, what level of authority and influence do you want to achieve within your field and what attributes do you want associated with your personal brand when someone thinks of you or talks about you to others?

If you became an authority or go-to person in your industry, what specific area of excellence, special attributes or specialist knowledge and expertise would differentiate you from other people in your industry? What level of authority and influence would you have within your organisation, with your industry peers and within your business networks?

If you were able to shape your desired brand reputation in the minds of others, what would they say about you when you're not in the room? What three words would come up in the same sentence as your name?

When thinking about and writing down what you want to be known for, use these criteria:

- Write your responses in the first person ('I' and 'My' statements).
- Write it like it's already happened; so this future identity starts to filter into your subconscious.
- Write it so it can be measured; if it's too vague you'll have trouble conjuring a vivid picture and difficulty knowing when it's been achieved.

Here are some examples to spark your thinking:

- I am one of Australia's foremost experts on <insert industry category> and renowned for <insert specialist problem-solving expertise>.
- I am an accredited <insert practitioner status> working at the cutting edge of <insert profession> and renowned for <insert specialist problem-solving expertise>.
- I am the CEO of a global <insert industry type> company leading the world in the <insert problem-solving> space. As a leader, I am renowned for <insert leadership qualities/values>
- I run one of Australia's top <insert profession> businesses. I am renowned for <insert specialist problem-solving expertise> among <insert niche or micro niche>.
- I am the owner of a seven-figure <insert profession> practice and have a reputation for <insert specialist problem-solving expertise>.
- I am an in-demand global <insert profession> working six months a year in Australia and six months a year in Europe. I am renowned for my work in <insert specialist area> with <insert niche or micro niche>.
- I am an internationally-recognised leader in <my industry> and renowned for my work in <insert specialist area>.

What do you want to be associated with?

Brand associations are the traits, attributes, benefits, ideas and other characteristics that come to mind when people think about a particular brand. When you think of Lego for example, brand associations that come to mind could be attributes such as bricks, colour, play, fun, building, children and learning.

Brand associations are fundamental in shaping others' thought processes and shaping your desired reputation over time. And while you may be clear about how you want people to perceive you, how does that become reality? You can't assume that people perceive you as you perceive yourself.

First, you need to understand where your personal brand is now in terms of brand associations. Then you can build a brand that generates the desired associations.

Create a catalogue of attributes

List your personal attributes in the following key areas:

- **Talents and traits** – innate abilities and strengths
- **Skills** – learned competencies
- **Superpowers** – special talents, skills or strengths you're renowned for
- **Specialist expertise** – specialist know-how that solves a problem
- **Personality** – personal qualities, preferences, energy, habits and tendencies
- **Character** – beliefs, morals, virtues and values
- **Benefits and results** – the difference you make through your work
- **Education** - qualifications, training and accreditations
- **Experience** – significant projects, experiences and achievements

- **Stories** – narratives in your name that convey meaning about your identity and value
- **Awards** – study, work or industry related

Describe your attributes

Next, develop a list of adjectives or key phrases that describe your most desirable personal brand attributes in a nutshell. You can use combinations, such as 'professional and approachable', 'progressive and practical', 'visionary and pragmatic' or 'intellectual and quick-witted'.

Or you can create a statement that includes the area in which you excel, such as 'a transformational customer service leader who is compassionate while also being results-driven'.

Test your perception

It's important to assess whether the view you have of yourself lines up with how others perceive you. Speaking with people whose opinion you value and who will give honest feedback is a good place to start, such as trusted team members, industry peers, mentors, leaders or friends. Ask them what words come to mind when they think of you and how they would describe you to someone else. These discussions will help you identify the gaps between how you are perceived and how you want to be perceived.

People and planet vision

What difference do you want to make?

The second part of a personal brand vision describes the kind of future you want to create for clients, the organisation you work for, the community in which you operate or the world as a whole, through your work. This externally-focused outcome is, in effect, an expression of optimism for a brighter future. It is about how a personal brand intends to create a ripple effect to change lives, to improve community outcomes, to move humanity forward through their Inner Brilliance. It is, therefore, their mark on the world, their legacy.

For a business owner, their aspirational vision may describe the kind of future they want to create for their clients through the product or service they deliver. For a community leader, their aspirational vision may describe the kind of life they want to create for their constituents in the place they live.

When personal brands make clear the difference they seek to make in the world through their vision, it helps their customers understand what they stand for, and helps the teams they lead answer the question, 'why are we here?'.

When a personal brand articulates their legacy through a compelling vision they become a purpose-driven leader. Leaders with a compelling vision aligned with a higher purpose attract people into their sphere who resonate with this kind of future.

If you're looking for some inspiration for considering your personal brand legacy, the United Nations' Sustainable Development Goals[24] are a good place to start. These goals, set in 2015 by the General Assembly of the United Nations, are a call to action by all countries to address a range of global challenges related to poverty, inequality, climate, environmental degradation, prosperity and peace.

The 17 goals with 169 targets are designed to stimulate action to achieve transformational outcomes in key areas of critical importance for humanity and the planet by 2030.

While there is an expectation that governments will take ownership and establish national frameworks to achieve these goals, there is much that private businesses and, indeed, individuals, can do by their decisions and actions. The goals can be used to derive inspiration for articulating your personal brand legacy.

Articulate the difference

When exploring the question of what difference you want to make, follow these criteria:

- Make it outward focused (for example, clients, other people, local community, environment).
- The outcome must solve a problem.
- Use optimistic language that is both aspirational and inspirational.

Here are some examples to spark your thinking:

- I've helped more than 10,000 people to overcome <insert problem> and <insert transformation>.
- Through my <insert signature methodology> I've helped more than 1,000 <insert client> to <insert outcome>.
- As a <insert type> leader, I've helped more than 100 <insert client> to achieve <insert result>.

Set a time period

Personal brand visions can also be written for specific periods of time, which could align with incremental progress in your career. For instance, if you are starting out in your career, you may set a five-year vision or you could set a five-, 10- and 20-year vision. In writing your time-bound vision, use the same formula, just add in the year or a specific date by which you want to achieve the vision.

For example:

- By 2030, I will be one of Australia's foremost experts on <insert industry category> and renowned for <insert specialist problem-solving expertise>. My work will change the lives of thousands of <insert niche or micro niche> by <insert transformation>.

There are many ways to express your personal brand vision. The key is to ensure that your personal brand vision statement is long enough to be meaningful to you and short enough to be memorable. Above all, ensure that your vision creates a vivid picture in your mind and describes what the result looks like. Keep your vision crystal clear so it can motivate and guide you in everyday decisions and actions.

Putting it all together

The next step is to combine the questions of 'what do you want to be known for?' – your professional standing – and 'what difference do you want to make?' – your planetary legacy – to craft your personal brand vision statement.

As an example, here's my personal brand vision:

- 'I am one of Australia's most respected authorities on brand communication and reputation. My Inner Brilliance Personal Branding™ system has helped more than 100,000 talented and ambitious professionals to build a strong personal brand and leave an indelible mark on the world.'

Here are some more examples:

- I am an internationally-recognised leader in <my industry> and renowned for my work in <insert specialist area>. My <insert signature methodology> is the cornerstone approach to <insert niche> and has helped more than 100,00 people to <insert outcome>.
- I am the CEO of a global <insert industry type> company leading the world in the <insert profession> space. Through our research, we've helped more than one million people to <insert outcome>

Now, it's your turn.

> ### *Activity – craft your personal brand vision statement*
>
> Create a personal brand vision that articulates how your Inner Brilliance will propel your professional standing while also leaving the world a better place through your legacy.
>
> - What do you want to be known for in your industry?
>
>   _____
>   _____
>   _____
>
> - What attributes do you want associated with your personal brand?
>
>   _____
>   _____
>   _____
>
> - What difference do you want to make?
>
>   _____
>   _____
>   _____
>
> - My personal brand vision statement is...
>
>   _____
>   _____
>   _____

Positioning – Differentiate your personal brand

Embrace what makes you different, get clear on what you stand for as a personal brand (your values) and define your specialist problem-solving expertise (your value) that delivers measurable value to those whom you serve.

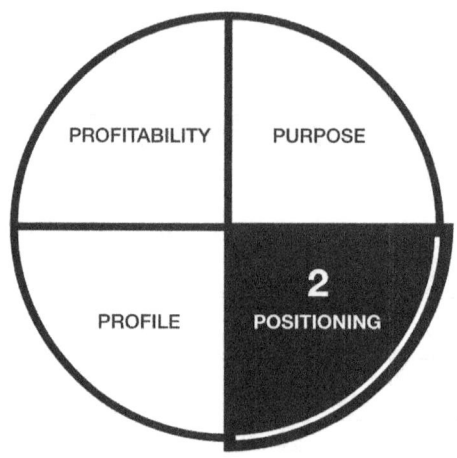

Step 3: Values – Uphold your standards

> 'There are three constants in life ...
> change, choice and principles.'
> Stephen Covey, American educator, author, businessman and speaker

Principles

The importance of core values

Our core values dictate what we deem important and strive to uphold at all times. In our career and business life, core values are the pillars of our personal brand, and the guideposts by which we make decisions, determine priorities and take action. Core values are also fundamental to our marketing program. They highlight what our personal brand stands for, acting as a beacon for prospective employers and clients.

Examples of core values include love, leadership, wisdom, accountability, growth, quality, fun, integrity, service, excellence, culture, diversity, respect, empowerment, contribution, courage, generosity, community and the like.

In conducting research for his book *Good to Great*, Jim Collins found that core values, like purpose, were essential for shifting from a company with good results to an enduring company of iconic stature, stating that, 'Enduring great companies preserve their core values and purpose while their business strategies and operating practices endlessly adapt to a changing world. This is the magical combination of preserve the core and stimulate progress'.[25]

Collins's contention that a core ideology, embodying a core purpose beyond making profit and core values, is a fundamental pillar to guide decisions and inspire people, and upon which to build a great organisation. It is the same with personal brands; holding firm to a consistent set of core values will stand you in good stead through an ever-changing marketplace and ever-changing expectations. When you are steadfast on your core values, by speaking and acting in alignment with them, you take the guesswork away – people trust you for your word because your principles have become the yardsticks by which you have become known.

When we speak and behave in line with our core values, we are more likely to feel happy and true to ourselves. However, if we say things and act in ways not congruent with our core values, we can feel unsettled and unauthentic. It can also affect our relationships with others who may perceive we've been fake or dishonest.

Making clear your core values is an important element of building a personal brand. You want to be transparent with your core values so people know what you stand for. If, however, you act out of alignment with your core values with a colleague or client, you will lose credibility and trust, and damage your reputation. That's why when detemining your personal brand core values, ask yourself, 'What am I not prepared to compromise on, ever?'.

Explore your values

Take some time to consider the core values that will best guide you in life and business. Here's a quick and simple way to identify your top core values:

1. List three people you most admire.
2. What do you most admire about these individuals that they represent in their everyday work and life?
3. Which of these attributes / values could you embody as part of your personal brand?

Below is a list of words that can reflect values. While the list is not exhaustive, it is a starting point to identify values that may be important to your personal brand.

Accuracy	Contribution	Fulfillment	Love	Punctuality	Understanding
Achievement	Cooperation	Generosity	Loyalty	Purposefulness	Uniqueness
Adaptability	Courage	Gentleness	Maturity	Quality	Value
Adventure	Creativity	Good attitude	Method	Resourcefulness	Versatility
Affection	Customer service	Gratitude	Meticulousness	Respect	Victory
Alertness	Dependability	Growth	Modesty	Responsibility	Vigor
Ambition	Determination	Happiness	Naturalness	Satisfaction	Warmth

Assertiveness	Diligence	Hard work	Nurturing	Security	Willpower
Authenticity	Dynamism	Health	Openness	Self actualisation	Wisdom
Balance	Education	Humour	Optimism	Sensibility	Wit
Beauty	Effectiveness	Homeliness	Organisation	Simplicity	Youthfulness
Benevolence	Efficiency	Honesty	Originality	Sincerity	Zeal
Boldness	Energy	Hope	Patience	Skill	
Calmness	Engagement	Humility	Peace	Sociability	
Capability	Enjoyment	Imagination	Perseverance	Specialness	
Capacity	Enterprise	Impartiality	Personal fulfillment	Status	
Career	Enthusiasm	Independence	Personal mastery	Strength	
Caring	Excellence	Innovation	Playfulness	Success	
Clear thinking	Faith	Integrity	Pleasantness	Sympathy	
Compassion	Fitness	Joviality	Politeness	Tact	
Competence	Flexibility	Joy	Practicality	Talent	
Confidence	Focus	Kindness	Precision	Teamwork	
Conscientious	Forgiveness	Knowledge	Professionalism	Tenacity	
Consideration	Freedom	Leadership	Progress	Thankfulness	
Contentment	Friendship	Learning	Prosperity	Thoroughness	

Embody your values

Core values expressed as actionable standards of behaviour make it easy for your colleagues and clients to know what to expect when working or doing business with you. This can include the expected approach to customer service, expected way of communicating, expected standard of performance and so on.

Some examples to spark your thinking

Here's some examples of how personal brand core values can be turned into actionable statements:

- **Customer excellence** – I go the extra yard to delight
- **Trust** – I do what I say I will
- **Value** - I create value for my customers at every touch point
- **Care** – I am kind and show empathy
- **Growth** – I learn and apply something new every day
- **Accountability** – I take responsibility and follow through
- **Innovation** – I am curious, creative and learn from trying new things
- **Relationships** – I put trust at the centre of relationships
- **Efficiency** – I do more with less
- **Integrity** – I am honest and ethical
- **Fun** – I go lightly and laugh out loud

When you turn your personal brand core values into actionable statements, they become the yardsticks by which you think, speak and act. When applied consistently, these core values become the 'trademark behaviours' by which you are known and, ultimately, drive a strong and positive reputation for your personal brand.

Activity – define your core values and trademark behaviours

1. Write down a list of values that resonate deeply within you.

   _____

   _____

   _____

   _____

   _____

2. Condense the list down to three to five values that, above all others, you would never compromise on.

   _____

   _____

   _____

   _____

3. Turn each value into an actionable statement that you want to become the trademark behaviours that you are known for.

   _____

   _____

   _____

   _____

Philosophy

Your personal brand philosophy is connected to your beliefs. Like core values, your beliefs govern your decisions, attitudes and behaviour, but they are different. Our philosophical beliefs are our convictions, or assumptions about life or business, that we accept to be true. Examples of beliefs include: 'blood is thicker than water' or 'lying is bad'. Beliefs are formed from myriad sources, including our parents, cultural upbringing, religion and education.

You will have beliefs about your area of expertise or your industry developed through your experiences at different workplaces and through the influence of different leaders, mentors and colleagues. For instance, as a result of my experience as a public relations and marketing professional, I believe that 'purpose, core values and vision are necessary pillars of effective brand communication'.

Most, if not all, professionals, are philosophers to some degree, with a philosophical position on their industry, profession or service. Throughout our careers, education and life experiences, and in pursuit of our own identities, we have searched, considered, validated, verified, debated and defended our thoughts and ideas in the name of what we believe. We have taken these thoughts and ideas and created our own bodies of knowledge – our philosophies – which we have then developed into a system, a methodology, a program, a training, a service.

This explains the many different approaches professionals use in their daily work. Consider the different philosophical positions that underpin different methodologies and approaches to medicine, child psychology, school teaching, nutrition, personal training, financial planning, childcare, insurance broking, accounting, marketing, and the list goes on.

In fact, it is these philosophical differences that set one practitioner apart from another and influence consumer choice. To this end, the philosophical approach of a professional can become their competitive advantage because consumers will often choose their preferred provider based on values and beliefs alignment.

An example of a personal brand philosophy is Richard Branson…

Sir Richard Branson is known as an optimistic entrepreneur who pushes the status quo by creating innovative solutions to customer problems and delivering an exceptional customer experience. His book *Screw it, Let's Do it*[26] sums up his philosophy on life and business. With chapters headings like 'Just Do it!', 'Have Fun!', 'Be Bold', 'Challenge Yourself', 'Stand on Your Own Feet' and 'Live in the Moment' exuding a 'say-yes-and-work-out-how-later philosophy', it's no surprise that staff at Virgin call him 'Dr Yes'.

Activity – craft your philosophy

Craft your philosophical standpoint or perspective on business, your industry or specialist area of expertise.

- Finish this sentence: I believe that…

_____

_____

_____

_____

Step 4: Value – Niche your expertise

'Strive not to be a success, but rather, to be of value'
Albert Einstein, German physicist, Nobel Prize winner

Your value is determined by how well you solve a problem a market is willing to pay for. In essence, your value is the unique specialist problem-solving expertise you possess that takes your customer from where they are now to where they want to be. The extent to which you add value, whether it be by solving your client's problem, navigating your team through change or nurturing stakeholder relationships, is one of the most important elements in achieving career success. Articulating the tangible and intangible value you contribute is a key part of cultivating your personal brand.

When defining the value you deliver, it is vital to understand that not all value is created equal. This is because value, like the concepts of beauty, art or success, means different things to different people. For instance, let us suppose I value 'timeliness' and 'affordable' pricing, I may choose to buy a plain watch from the local variety store. However, if I value 'timeliness' and 'prestige', I may choose to buy a Rolex watch from a specialist watch store in the city. While both watches will tell the time equally well, clearly the purchase decision is influenced by what I value most.

Problem

Your ability to solve customer problems is your value

In today's competitive and commoditised global marketplace, it is more important than ever for individuals to articulate the specific value they deliver if they want to cut through the noise and attract their target market. And while many professionals know what they do, many struggle to articulate the true value they provide to their customer and organisation as a whole.

The purpose of a product / service is to solve a customer problem (to meet a need, alleviate a pain point or fulfil a desire or want). In effect, customers are looking for the right person or product who can take them from A, where they are now stuck in their problem to B, where they want to be in the future with their problem solved.

The extent to which a person will pay for the right solution to their problem depends on how big the problem is to them. The bigger the problem, the higher the value a person will place on finding the right solution (product / service). This is because the person has a greater motivation to find relief from the unease, tension or discomfort they attribute to their current (problem) situation and move to a place of comfort, pleasure and internal equilibrium in their desired future (problem-free) state.

When you can articulate the distinct value of the solution you deliver through your specialist knowledge and expertise, you will connect with your target market in a very powerful way.

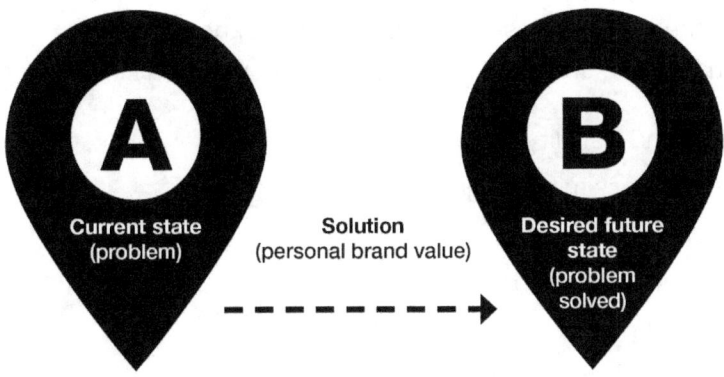

The space between A and B is the **gap** between a person's current problem state and their desired future problem-free state. Your personal brand value is the solution that closes the gap.

Know your customer's currency

When thinking about the customer gap you close, consider it from the perspective of their desired outcome. For instance, do they want more time, visibility, wealth, confidence, influence, connection, trust or leads? In essence, this is your client's currency; what they value most and what they are paying in exchange for your unique value offering/ solution. For example, a customer's currency could be engagement, performance, income, influence or confidence.

Let's say my client's currency is confidence; that is, they want more confidence. My value then, is how well I solve my client's confidence gap – the chasm between where they are now, feeling self-doubt and fearful and focused on mistakes and failure to where they want to be, feeling worthy and optimistic and focused on learning and success.

Here's another example. Through my consulting practice, I close the 'customer connection' gap for small business clients struggling to attract their ideal client. I close this gap by transforming their marketing content and collateral from dull and detached to energised and engaging. This helps their marketing messages cut through the noise and resonate more deeply with those they want to connect with.

What's the gap you close with your specialist knowledge and expertise? Here are some examples to spark your thinking:

- brand visibility gap
- business mindset gap
- prosperity gap
- confidence gap
- trust gap
- theory-practice gap
- resilience gap
- communication gap
- learning gap
- influence gap
- leadership gap
- innovation gap
- engagement gap
- culture gap
- lead generation gap
- courage gap

In closing your customer's currency gap, your value is also as a catalyst of change in facilitating the transformative process – this is a superpower! Whether you solve the problem completely or are an important link in a chain of people who solve the problem, you play a valuable part in the ultimate outcome for the customer. The customer service officer who transfers the customer enquiry to the right person to answer the question is just as valuable as the person who answers the question. The value is in helping progress the customer from current (problem) state to desired future (problem-free) state.

> ### *Activity – identify your customer's currency gap*
>
> - What is the currency gap you close for each niche you serve?
>
> _____
>
> _____
>
> _____
>
> _____
>
> _____
>
> _____
>
> _____
>
> _____

Understand your customer's current state and desired future state

Once you understand your customer's currency gap, you need to analyse how the problem currently impacts their business / life and how they envision their business / life being once the problem is solved.

Problems negatively impact a person's business / life, both logically and emotionally. Problems solved positively impact a person's business / life, both logically and emotionally. The value of your solution is what transforms the logical and emotional factors from negative to positive. This concept is shown in the figure below.

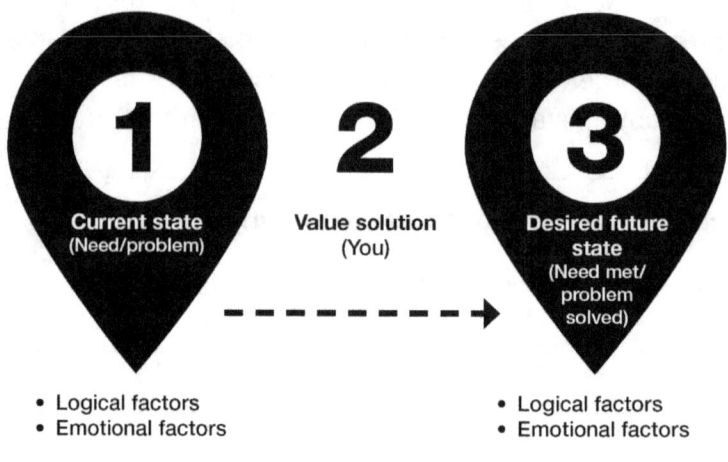

©Ros Weadman

For example, a small business owner behind in their bookkeeping could have cashflow and debt problems (logical) and this makes them feel stressed and fearful (emotional). Once the small business owner finds the right bookkeeper and gets their paperwork up-do-date they could have good cash flow and pay their bills on time (logical), and this makes them feel happy and have peace of mind (emotional).

Here's another example. Let's say a person is looking for a personal trainer because they are overweight and unfit, and this is negatively impacting their life. Their current (problem) state might be that they have high blood pressure, interrupted sleep and none of their clothes fit anymore (logical factors). This makes them feel unhappy and insecure (emotional factors). They are therefore willing to pay for a personal trainer with the right training solution (value) who can help them achieve their goal in the most efficient and effective way possible. Once they achieve their weight and fitness goals (problem solved), they will be physically healthier and sleep better (logical factors) and will feel happier and more confident (emotional factors).

> ***Activity – understand your customer's current state and desired future state***
>
> To articulate the true value of the solution you provide, you must understand how your client's problem is affecting them now, logically and emotionally, and how they will be affected logically and emotionally when they are free of their problem in the future.
>
> **Current**
>
> - What is your client experiencing logically and emotionally in their current problem state?
>
> _____
>
> _____
>
> _____
>
> _____
>
> _____
>
> **Future**
>
> - What will your client experience logically and emotionally in their future problem-free state after using/experiencing your valuable solution?
>
> _____
>
> _____
>
> _____
>
> _____
>
> _____

Identify the types of value in your solution

In solving your customer's problem, your personal brand value has three key dimensions:

- the **product/service value** associated with your specialist knowledge and expertise
- the **performance value** that delivers results for your customer
- the **personal value** that nurtures the customer relationship.

The below table give examples of these three types of value.

Product/service value	Performance value	Personal value
For example: • Features • Quality • Market differentiation • Degree of customisation • Mode of delivery • Guarantees / warranties • After-sales service • Reputation • Specialist expertise	For example: • Increased revenue • Time saved • Increased efficiency • Fewer sick days • Increased staff retention • Increased productivity • Increased leads • Reduced cost of goods sold • Increased visibility	For example: • Onboarding process • Degree of personalisation • Customer relationship management • Trust and respect • Confidentiality

Use the below table to articulate the three types of value you deliver as a personal brand.

Activity: Identify the product, performance and personal value of your solution.		
Product/service value	**Performance value**	**Personal value**

Proposition

Now it's time to articulate a personal brand value proposition that encompasses how your unique value solution solves your customer's problem by closing the gap between their current state and desired future state. To do this, we need to identify your personal brand's most valuable attribute in the eyes of the customer.

A powerful way of doing this is to define a signature value anthem for your personal brand. This is a short phrase that captures the essence of your most distinctive and significant competitive advantage and is of highest value to your customers. This is your area of performance excellence which gives the single biggest benefit to your customers.

One of the best ways to define your signature value anthem is to use a two-or-three-word phrase. A two-word phrase works best using an adjective for an emotional modifier followed by a noun to describe the brand function, such as 'inspiring communication', 'authentic leadership' or 'innovative engineering'.

A three-word phrase works best as an adjective, noun, noun combination where the adjective is an emotional modifier, the first noun is a descriptive modifier and the second noun is a brand function.

Here are some examples:

- Jacinda Ardern – compassionate political leadership
- Pink – acrobatic musical stagecraft
- Madonna – rebellious musical fantasy
- Olivia-Newton John – wholesome musical ballads

My signature value anthem is 'resonant brand communication' based on my purpose-driven and values-based content, strategies and methodologies designed to engage hearts and minds at the deepest level. 'Resonant brand communication', is therefore, my highest brand value, my key competitive advantage, my most distinguishing attribute, my area of greatest performance.

What is the single biggest benefit you bring to your customers, your most significant competitive advantage? It could be found in a variety of service areas such as leadership, strategy, relationships, prosperity, wellbeing, vision, education, service or it could be a particular product attribute or unique feature, a methodology or technological innovation, for example.

Here's a simple, five-step process to help you craft a personal brand value proposition, encompassing your signature value anthem.

1. Identify the **target market**
2. Clarify the **problem**, logically and emotionally
3. Define your **value solution**, with signature value anthem
4. Specify the **ultimate outcome**; the problem solved logically and emotionally
5. Include a **proof point**

Here is an example, using a bookkeeper who has defined their signature value anthem as 'meticulous financial standards':

> *I help small business owners* **(1. target market)** *overwhelmed with paperwork and frustrated by poor cash flow* **(2. problem, with logical and emotional factors)**.
>
> *I'm an accredited bookkeeper with meticulous financial standards, a value-based pricing model and cloud technology* **(3. value solution)**. *I'll get your business books and invoicing up-to-date within 14 days, giving you peace of mind and freeing up your time so you can get on with running your business.* **(4. Outcome, with logical and emotional factors)**.
>
> *One of my recent clients saved over $2,000 a month in lost time chasing up unpaid invoices* **(5. proof point)**.

Activity – craft your personal brand value proposition

Use the below prompts to create your signature value proposition.

Five-step signature value proposition process:

1. Identify the **target market**
2. Clarify the **problem** (logical and emotional factors)
3. Define the **value solution**, including signature value anthem
4. Specify the **outcome** (logical and emotional factors)
5. Include a **proof** point, if possible.

My Signature Value Proposition is…

_____

_____

_____

_____

_____

Pitch

Your personal brand value proposition can be used effectively on a website and on marketing collateral but is too wordy for a casual conversation when answering the 'So, what do you do?' question.

How you answer the question 'what do you do for a living?' or 'what business are you in?' makes a difference to how people perceive you and whether it leads to engaging conversation or polite but superficial chit-chat.

You'll seem more interesting and spark more curiosity in the other person if you include the outcome of what you do in the answer.

If you respond with your job title / profession ('I'm an engineer') or product / service ('I sell shoes') only, you won't sound as interesting, evoke as strong a reaction or resonate as deeply as when you add the difference you make in people's lives through your work.

Revlon International Corporation's Charles Revlon famously once said, 'In the factory we make cosmetics. In the department stores we sell hope'.

How do you make your customers look, feel or live better through your work? In other words, what is the human-centred outcome you deliver?

Here's a few ideas from some of my favourite small business brands (including some of my clients):

- 'I'm an audiologist. I help people connect with loved ones and fully participate in life through the gift of improved hearing'.
- 'I'm a dentist. My practice specialises in giving people the smile of their dreams.'
- 'I'm a physiotherapist. I free up peoples' bodies so they regain their mobility, independence and confidence, and can lead a more fulfilling life.'
- 'I run a recruitment company. We pride ourselves on matching the right person to the right role and organisation for a sustained working partnership.'
- 'I'm a hairdresser. Clients leave my salon with a spring in their step because of their renewed confidence in how they look.'
- 'I run a female-owned domestic and commercial painting company. We're an industry trailblazer because we empower women to shake the mould of the typical tradie.'
- 'I'm a property investor strategist. I help people achieve financial independence, have choice in retirement and to leave a legacy.'

By focusing on how you help rather than on what you do makes for a far more interesting conversation. So, next time you're at a barbecue or striking up a conversation with someone new, rather than just saying 'I'm a <area of expertise>', say 'I'm a <area of expertise>, I help <insert name of target market> to achieve/feel <difference you make>'.

Now, I'm both interested and intrigued, 'please tell me more'.

Profile – Promote your personal brand

Build your visibility in the marketplace, extend your professional network and increase your newsworthiness so you become a credible and trusted authority in your industry.

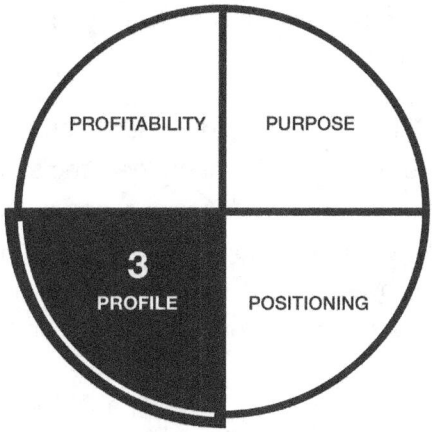

Step 5: Voice – Communicate your personality

'The art of communication is the language of leadership.'
James C. Humes, American author and presidential speechwriter

Your personal brand voice is your brand's personality brought to life through the unique combination of words and tonality that convey your brand story and core message to the world. Brand voice projects your personal brand's authentic character, style and attitude and is underpinned by your personal brand purpose, values, beliefs and vision. Brand voice must run consistently across all customer touchpoints and marketing platforms and mediums.

Personal brand narrative

A personal brand narrative communicates who you are, what you do, why you do it and how you do it. It contains your personal value proposition and, potentially, case studies that highlight your specialist problem-solving intelligence in action. The narrative is written in relatable language and using words and tonality that align with your individual style and attitude.

Joseph Campbell's 'Hero's Journey', discussed earlier, is a brilliant structure for brand storytelling. As mentioned, the storyline involves a hero who goes on an adventure, faces challenges, learns valuable lessons, wins a victory and, with newfound insights, returns home transformed. Many movies follow this familiar pattern, such as *Star Wars*, *The Wizard of Oz*, *The Matrix*, Clarke in *Superman* and the Harry Potter series.

While there are different versions of the Hero's Journey template, there are typically 12 stages in three parts, as follows:

- **Part 1 – The Comfortable Old World**

    1. **The ordinary world** – what life was like beforehand, the status quo
    2. **The call to adventure** – the problem, challenge or threat that confronts or interrupts the hero's life and threatens to take them out their comfort zone
    3. **Refusal of the call** – at first there was hesitation and reluctance by the hero as the journey is perceived to be risky
    4. **Meeting the mentor** – then someone the hero looked up to comes onto the scene and gives them inspiration, wisdom or practical help for the journey
    5. **Crossing the threshold** – the hero leaves on their journey

- **Part 2 – The Quest Adventure**

    1. **Tests, battles and chaos/allies and enemies** – the trials and tribulations experienced by the hero and where they learn their lessons
    2. **Approach the inner cave** – the hero enters the most dangerous part of the new realm, such as the villain's lair or their own mind of negative self-talk
    3. **The ordeal** – the hero faces the biggest test of all, confronts their greatest fear
    4. **Seize the reward** – the hero is now ready to grasp their reward, the new knowledge, object, way of life

- **Part 3 – The Newfound World**

    1. **The road back home** – the hero tries to return to the normal world but there are more dangers to tackle
    2. **Resurrection, atonement** – the final test or ordeal the hero faces which they must survive to have their happy ending
    3. **Return with the elixir** – the hero returns home with the prize – knowledge, object or insight. They have changed because of the journey and are a better person for it.

The Hero's Journey storyline is particularly powerful as a personal brand story template for coaches, consultants and advisors who, through their practice, may be working with clients who have been through a similar life experience. For example, the weight loss consultant who struggled with their weight since childhood, trying every diet, until one day later in the life they connect with a health consultant who gives them an insight that changes their entire thinking around food and diets, and transforms their life. They then use their newfound wisdom and specific philosophical approach to help others going through the same struggles.

If you like the Hero's Journey model for brand storytelling but find it challenging to create a story that uses all 12 stages, consider using a shorter version of the model, ensuring to maintain the three-part base structure. Below is an alternative version of the Hero's Journey with some key questions to consider when crafting your personal brand story.

> ### *Activity – Craft your personal brand story*
>
> Craft your personal brand story using this simplified version of the Hero's journey framework.
>
> **Part 1 – Old World**
>
> - What was work, business or life like before you made the change?
>
> _____
>
> _____
>
> _____
>
> - What was the problem, challenge, frustration, need in your work, business or life that presented itself and had to be resolved?
>
> _____
>
> _____
>
> _____
>
> - Who in your life came along and inspired you to seek the solution to the problem, challenge, frustration or need?
>
> _____
>
> _____
>
> _____

- If there was no person or mentor, what was the defining moment when you made the decision to seek a better way of doing things?

___

___

___

Part 2 – The Quest

- What fears and challenges – internally and externally - did you face in the journey of seeking to overcome the problem?

___

___

___

___

- What lessons did you learn along the way?

___

___

___

___

- What was the ultimate insight, realisation or epiphany you had because of confronting the various fears and challenges? Perhaps the insight came to you because of a customer experience, a technological discovery, a process improvement, a conversation with a mentor or an industry wisdom, for example.

___

___

___

___

Part 3 – New World

- How did the insight change your thinking, beliefs or values, and what was the ultimate transformation for you?

  _____
  _____
  _____

- How are you now using the elixir – the newfound knowledge or insight– to bring value to your clients through your product, service or programs?

  _____
  _____
  _____

- What is the brand promise you now deliver to your customers?

  _____
  _____
  _____

Apply Aristotelian wisdom to your personal brand narrative

When constructing your personal brand narrative, it's useful to keep in mind the wisdom of two and a half millennia ago when Aristotle said that impactful rhetoric – speaking designed to persuade an audience – has three components:

- **Logos** – an appeal to logic, to convince an audience based on reason
- **Pathos** – an appeal to emotions, to convince an audience by invoking feelings, an empathy for the argument

- **Ethos** – an appeal to ethics, to convince an audience of the credibility of the person making the argument.

The logos of your brand story captures the logical part of the mind through rationality, grounded reasoning, facts and figures, and evidence.

The pathos of your brand story evokes feelings by using specific language and tonality to answer the 'why' question (why you do what you do) and articulate what you stand for and why it matters.

The ethos of your brand story provides evidence of your credibility, reliability, trustworthiness, expertise and authority.

When you build logos, pathos and ethos into your brand story, you give meaning to the 'why' that sits behind your 'what' and 'how'. The resultant emotional connection becomes a motivational force to fulfil your purpose and achieve your goals, and magnetic pull for others who resonate with your beliefs and values.

This is why your brand story must align with, and have embedded within it, your core values and beliefs and, ideally, link to your personal story. For instance, I have a strong belief that brands with a compelling outward-focused vision have the power to achieve a positive difference in their local communities, towns, nation or the world, beyond that which they deliver for their customer. I want to see a world where more business owners are empowered to think bigger picture and stand for something beyond their product/service. This lines up with my personal story of wanting to use my passion and talent for communication to be a catalyst for positive change.

Have a core message

Every personal brand needs an overarching core message, linked to their narrative, that they want to convey to the world. Your core message could be two or three words only, it could be a short phrase or it could be a sentence or two. It can be a call to action, describe the outcome you deliver or be a voice of inspiration. Most often, it is connected to your purpose and vision.

To illustrate, here are some core messages that defined the personal brands who delivered them:

'I have a dream that someday this nation will live up to its creed that all men are created equal.' Dr Martin Luther King Jr

'You must be the change you want to see in the world.'
Mahatma Ghandi

'All you need is love.' John Lennon

'Brands with purpose and vision move humanity forward.'
Ros Weadman

Personal Presentation

Your personal presentation style, including your hair, make-up, clothing and accessories, are also vitally important aspects of personal branding and should align with your personality. For instance, if your personality is sunny and vibrant, then wearing a colourful wardrobe could be congruent. This, however, doesn't mean you go out and buy a new wardrobe of clothes featuring flowers of every colour of the rainbow because you think it will match your personality.

Personal presentation and styling is an industry on its own and is not explored in this book. I do, however, recommend you seek an accredited image consultant if this is an area in which you need advice.

Feeling confident and comfortable in your personal styling is especially important when it comes to having professional photos done for your social media profiles and website and/or videography for your speaker showreel.

Persuasion

How likeable are you?

As previously mentioned, personal branding accelerates the know, like and trust process. Because you are proactively positioning your personal brand, building a profile and shaping a reputation, people may feel they know you before they meet you. But when they do meet you, either in person, over the phone or online, the likeability factor comes home to roost.

As creatures driven by deep-seated survival mechanisms to fit in and not be ostracised by the 'tribe' or social group, likeability is an important attribute of nurturing relationships and establishing partnerships. A great piece of advice I received was to 'be easy to buy from and easy to work with'. The latter goes to the heart of likeability; that is, being perceived as friendly, approachable, able to build rapport easily, having empathy and being personally relatable.

There are many elements that contribute to someone being perceived as likeable and building rapport; body language being among the most important. Particular gestures, for example, can either enhance or detract from the rapport-building process. For instance, crossing your limbs in a closed posture can discourage someone from striking up a conversation with you whereas using open gestures such as opening your arms to welcome someone into a group is more likely to result in people perceiving you more favourably.

The use of body language is central to Dr Robert Cialdini's laws of influence outlined in his book *Influence: the psychology of persuasion*[27]; particularly, the law of likeability. The law of likeability is based on the notion that people prefer to say yes to someone they like. A sense of familiarity, warmth and security comes from dealing with someone we view as similar or instinctively like, even though we may not know them.

While body language plays an important role in someone's 'likeability' factor, we also like people based on a number of attributes, including their personality, language, ability to listen and focus on us. Liking can also extend to how attractive they are perceived to be.

The phenomenon of people liking good-looking people is what social scientists call the 'halo effect'. It occurs when one positive aspect of a person dominates the way people view them. Research shows if someone is viewed as attractive, we automatically assign them other favourable attributes, such as talent, honesty, intelligence and kindness.

Likeability is particularly important for personal brands pursuing a career in politics. In fact, likeability is often the key deciding factor for some voters in the absence of, or care for, other factors such as policy stance. It is important to note, however, that likeability and influence don't always correlate. As international personal branding professor Talaya Waller[28] found, Hilary Clinton did not win the 2016 US Presidential election against the more likeable and self-made celebrity, Donald Trump, but her historic loss influenced more women to run for political office.

How to influence with authority

The law of authority – another of Dr Robert Cialdini's six laws of influence - can help you shape people's perceptions and position you as an authority in your niche.

This law is based on the notion that people will tend to obey authority figures even if they disagree with what is being asked of them. People will often comply with requests from people who wear uniforms of the armed forces or emergency services, have titles such as professor or doctor, or have implied status through their use of other trappings of authority such as an expensive car.

Examples of the law of authority used in marketing include a television commercial for toothpaste showing a dentist dressed in a white coat, expensive leather seating in the waiting room of a prestige car dealership, valet parking at a hotel or an Olympic athlete endorsing a brand of runners.

Some ways you can use the law of authority as part of your personal brand, include:

- Dress like you are already a success because first impressions do still matter even in an increasingly online marketplace and hybrid workplace. Being well groomed, with hair, clothing and accessories that align with your personal style, give you that extra spring in your step from feeling confident and purposeful.
- When guest speaking, provide a biography that positions you as an authority in your niche. Rather than sounding like a résumé, a biography includes what makes you different from others in the field and why your message matters in the world, now.
- Use open body language to project confidence and certainty. Closed body language, such as crossed arms and legs and not looking straight at the audience, give an impression of uncertainty and lacking confidence.
- When speaking, use command tonality. Command tonality is when there is a downward inflection at the end of a sentence so it sounds more direct and emphatic. Questioning tonality, on the other hand, has an upward inflection. This sounds like you are seeking validation of your statement and can give the impression you are uncertain of your content.
- Include accreditations, qualifications and awards on your website and marketing material.

Persuasive presentations

Whether running a workshop, pitching to a potential client or delivering a presentation, connecting with an audience requires a presenter to have clarity of message, confidence in their presentation skills and congruence of voice tonality and body language. An understanding of the different learning styles of people can also help a presenter engage their audience.

Developed by Dr Bernice McCarthy in the late 1970s, the 4MAT model[29] provides a useful structure for developing a presentation and engaging an audience based on the following four key learning styles:

- People who want to know **Why** (imaginative learners who seek meaning and purpose, like to reflect and think bigger picture)
- People who want to know **What** (analytic learners who seek facts and figures, enjoy research and like to explore concepts)
- People who want to know **How** (practical learners who seek steps and formulas so they can experiment, build or create something)
- People who want to find out **What if** (dynamic learners who seek new perspectives, speculate possibility and evolve ideas to different scenarios)

While the 4MAT model has most commonly been used as a framework in training and teaching scenarios, it's also a useful structure for communicating in a variety of other situations such as presenting an idea, facilitating a brainstorming session or delivering a presentation.

Below is an overview of how to appeal to the four learning styles.

- **Why?**

    The 'why' frame establishes the purpose of the communication, the environmental context and why the issue / idea / occasion is important, significant, meaningful or relevant to the audience, community, humanity. To establish the 'why', use stories, benefits, quotes, questions, statistics, examples and the like, to create meaning around the topic of focus.

- **What?**

    The 'what' frame tells the audience what they need to know about the issue / idea / occasion. To establish the 'what', provide tangible information such as a definition, facts and figures, historical information, research statistics, case studies and the like, to create concepts and link relationships.

- **How?**

    The 'how' frame engages the audience to act. To establish the 'how', show the steps to be followed, consider options, brainstorm ideas, use hands-on activities, use hypothetical scenarios, identify tools and tactics, and operational procedures, to build skills.

- **What if?**

    The 'what if' frame engages the audience to consider how to apply the idea to the external world and into the future. To establish the 'what if', ask the audience to adapt the information to different scenarios, give an open-ended task, speculate a new application or refinement.

While you couldn't know the learning styles of individuals in an audience, the 4MAT model is a valuable structure for preparing content that appeals to the diverse interests.

Improve the receptivity of your message

Everyone communicates but not everyone is heard. In today's overcommunicated world, people respond to what they care about and ignore everything else.

With people experiencing information overload and a bombardment of competing messages streaming daily from multiple platforms and devices, gaining people's attention has become a huge challenge for us all. And when you consider that people process information differently based on their personal beliefs, values, attitudes, sensory preferences and experiences, you can't assume that, even if your message has connected, that it's been interpreted as you intended.

Here are seven criteria to help your message resonate more deeply with the intended audience.

- **Have a purpose**

    Begin with the end in mind by asking yourself, 'what is the desired outcome of this message?' Is it to inform? educate? persuade? engage? inspire? advocate? change behaviour? A message delivered with intention will help you communicate your desired outcome without ambiguity.

- **Know your audience**

    Whether you're doing a keynote presentation, writing a blog or pitching a media release, audience-focused content is essential for effective communication. Here's some questions to help you get to know the audience better:

    - What are their values and beliefs about the topic?
    - What do they know about the topic?

- What don't they know about the topic?
- What are their present attitudes towards the topic?
- What is the level of impact of the topic on the audience?
- What are their aspirations in relation to the topic?
- What is their common language?

- **Own a position**

   To cut through the distraction, communication needs a central point, relevant to the audience. What is the core message you want to make that is of value or major benefit to the audience?

   Put your core message upfront, such as in the headline or first paragraph of an article, or in the first few sentences of a verbal presentation.

   Three-word core messages are particularly powerful. For example, 'reputation is critical!'.

- **Keep it simple**

   A message is more likely to connect with the audience if it is simple. Avoid using unnecessary technical jargon, acronyms and multiple syllable words when there is a simple alternative that conveys the same meaning.

- **Be congruent**

   Ensure congruence between verbal and non-verbal communication. This means that words, tone and body language need to be in sync to maintain credibility and impart the desired meaning.

- **Be creative**

   Use the rule of three

   The rule of three is based on the idea that three is the optimum number of points to form a pattern of information to aid memory retention. Some well-known examples are:

   'Friends, Romans, countrymen.'

   'The good, the bad and the ugly.'

   'Blood, sweat and tears.'

- **Appeal to the senses**

   In everyday language we use words associated with different senses – vision, hearing, taste, smell and touch – because this is how we, as humans, process information.

   Most often, people will prefer one sense over another, and this can influence our preferred language type. For example, visually-oriented people will use words associated with seeing (I see what you mean), auditory-oriented people will use words associated with hearing (I hear what you say) and kinaesthetically (touch)-oriented people will use words associated with touch or emotions (I feel I understand you).

   While you can't know the sensory preferences of an entire audience, if you choose words that appeal to the different sensory modalities, you'll have a greater chance of appealing to more people within the target audience.

- **Be consistent**

   To ensure a united voice and avoid confusion about what you stand for as a brand, apply your message consistently across all people, platforms and touchpoints connected with your brand.

Step 6: Visibility – Elevate your presence

> *'In a crowded marketplace, fitting in is a failure. In a busy marketplace, not standing out is the same as being invisible.'*
> Seth Godin, American author and marketing strategist

You may know you're great at what you do but that won't help you achieve your ambitions if no-one else knows. Building a personal brand is a strategic process and this is especially true when it comes to selecting the right promotional tools and tactics to deliver your message and connect with the right audiences.

Promotion

Choosing the right promotional mediums is important to ensure your message reaches your desired target markets and that you get the best return on your financial investment. Guessing the right combination of mediums to use to reach your target markets is akin to shooting arrows into the air hoping to hit a target. You could be wasting your time, money and effort if you don't accurately pinpoint your target.

By researching your customers thoroughly, you will discover where your target market 'hangs out' and how they prefer to consume information. What social media platforms do they regularly post on? Do they participate in specific social media forums? Do they read particular magazines? Do they attend certain business networking meetings? Do they attend trade shows or conferences? Do they prefer to receive text messages or emails or hard copy information?

Promotional techniques to elevate the profile of your personal brand can include traditional offline mediums such as a brochure, direct mail leaflet and sales letter; online mediums, such as a website, social media pages, business blog, internet advertising, mobile application, email and e-newsletter; and personal communications such as networking events, trade shows, personal selling and word-of-mouth marketing.

The following key promotional techniques can be used as part of an integrated marketing communications approach to raise awareness and extend your reach in the marketplace and to connect with customers.

- **Online marketing**

    Building a website to drive leads or make sales. It also includes landing pages (single page websites) used for the primary purpose of gathering contact details in exchange for a free offer. It also includes search engine optimisation to help the discovery of your website.

- **Social media marketing**

    Using social media channels such as Facebook, Twitter, LinkedIn, Instagram and the like to build a profile, engage audiences, advertise products and establish thought leadership. The channels chosen depend on where your target market hangs out.

- **Direct marketing**

    This includes unsolicited approaches such as bulk mail outs, cold calling and telemarketing or it can be on a permission-basis, such as emailing a list of subscribers.

- **Content marketing**

    The creation and sharing of online material such as videos, blogs and social media posts that does not explicitly promote a brand but is intended to stimulate interest in products or services or establish thought leadership.

- **Public relations**

    Public relations is about establishing and maintaining mutual understanding between an organisation and its internal and external publics. It is used to advance an agenda, influence perception, change behaviour, build public profile and protect, enhance or build reputations through the media, social media or self-produced communications. Unlike advertising, PR is usually through unpaid and earned methods.

- **Sales promotions**

    Usually one-off or deliberately timed tactical moves to stimulate buyer behaviour. Sales promotion strategies can include trial offers, time-limited discounts, seasonal sales, two-for-one offers and the like.

- **Advertising**

    This is a paid method of promotion and can include pay click advertising as well as newspaper, magazine, social media, cinema and signage advertising.

- **Marketing collateral**

    Includes promotional materials such as a whitepaper, brochure, flyer and information pack.

- **Branding**

    Brings your image to life through a logo, colour scheme, emblems, characters and the like. Branding can be applied to all marketing materials and touchpoints including websites, social media pages, vehicles, uniforms, signage and stationery.

- **Events**

    Events are in-person or online opportunities to bring together a desired target audience and can include webinars, seminars, workshops, masterclasses, trade shows, business breakfasts, special launches, openings and book signings.

- **Networking**

    Networking includes being a member of formal business groups and attending business events for the purpose of making new connections. Informal networking also occurs in online communities.

Publishing

Publishing high quality content is one of the most effective ways to increase awareness of your personal brand, build your credibility and position yourself as an authority. Publishing encompasses a broad range of activities, such as writing a book, blog, social post or newsletter, making videos or podcasts, or creating images, infographics and other visual elements.

Choosing the right platforms

Writing blogs, posts and articles, making videos and using technology in other creative ways to share your ideas and insights online is one of the most accessible ways to convey your message and demonstrate your expertise, and an effective way to build your visibility. When combined with search engine optimisation principles, you can enhance your rankings and become more easily found.

While publishing on relevant social media platforms is a plank of a personal branding visibility strategy, having a central repository of blogs and articles, such as a personal website or blog platform, is essential so your wisdom can be found easily and conveniently in one place.

If you're a professional, you need to be on LinkedIn; it's the social media platform for professionals where jobs are posted, recruiters do their research, industry groups and networks collaborate, and people share their ideas, insights and inspirations. LinkedIn is a golden opportunity to build your profile because at the time of writing, only a small percentage of active LinkedIn users create content. These are the people who are leveraging their personal brand the most effectively because their content is appearing in the feeds of their connections and followers as often as they commit to publishing it.

The social media channels you select to communicate with the target markets you wish to influence will depend on where your markets congregate. It's best to choose one or two social media channels and service them well rather than be on four or five channels and service them poorly. If you are a B2B business, you most likely need to be on LinkedIn and one other channel such as Facebook, Instagram, Tik Tok or Pinterest. If you're a B2C business you most likely need to be on Facebook, Instagram or other relevant channels.

While there is a myriad of social media channels, the table below provides some pointers for using some of the more popular channels.

Social Media	Key Information	Ways to Use it
LinkedIn	Different levels of membership provide different levels of visibility and access Individuals and organisations can set up a page Members share thoughts, experiences, third-party articles, educational opportunities, sales opportunities	Post insights, share links, write an article, use video, use the newsletter function, create a carousel Become a member of relevant groups then post insightful articles

Social Media	Key Information	Ways to Use it
Facebook	Users share experiences, thoughts, ideas, images, videos and links Users can take action such as 'like', 'share' or 'comment' Users connect by accepting 'friend requests' Users can set up groups (open or closed)	Develop a regular posting schedule and stick to it Use a combination of formats including video, images, links to interesting articles, inspiring quotes, comment on the latest news, post with a link to a blog on a website, cartoons, infographics and the like Gather information by listening to what people are talking about, ask questions to get feedback, run quick polls, use live video Participate in business groups, special interest groups Trial an advertising campaign
Instagram	Photo and video sharing platform	Post high quality images that are mobile-friendly Cross-post your images directly to other social media Use location tags to highlight the physical location of your business
X	Microblogging site	Announce blogs, new products, comment on latest news Follow relevant people
YouTube	Video sharing site	Post video content about your business and its products Make a series of 'how to' videos Make videos on customer success stories and case studies

Social Media	Key Information	Ways to Use it
Pinterest	A visual bookmarking tool that helps you discover and save creative ideas	Create theme-based pin boards Share images and videos of industry-related content Re-pin and like other content that suits your community

Tips for engaging on social media

Using social media is a great way to make connections, learn new things, share information and promote your products and services. Here are some ways to be more engaging and increase engagement on your social media sites.

- **Create valuable content**

    Create high quality content using the right key words to represent your brand and you'll rank online. Develop a basic content strategy by selecting three key content pillars relevant to your industry category then repurpose content to suit different channels.

- **Post consistently**

    Posting consistently is more important than frequency; so, choose a realistic posting schedule that you can commit to on your primary social media platform and stick to it.

- **Be genuine**

    Be yourself and write or speak in line with your values. It's okay to share your highs and lows, successes and failures, as your community will learn and gain valuable insights.

- **Use the 80/20 posting rule**

  Serve don't just sell. The 80/20 rule is 80 per cent educational and 20 per cent promotional content. This means that 80 per cent of the content is blogs, links to interesting articles and videos, tools, tips and the like, and 20 per cent is about how you can add value through your product or service.

- **Participate in communities**

  Create your own communities and join communities on Facebook, LinkedIn and other channels to make good network connections.

- **Be generous**

  Generosity is a wonderful marketing strategy. Become a 'go to' person for information on your subject area by sharing valuable insights and resources, for example, by creating a downloadable ebook or checklist.

- **Wrap your content in story**

  Stories are engaging and help people understand your message more clearly. Use metaphors, anecdotes and case studies to show how you solve customers' problems, celebrate client successes by sharing their good news and tell the story of your brand by creating an interesting video.

- **Write for a specific audience**

  Write with a specific audience in mind and have only one key message for them.

- **Use conversational language and plain English**

    Plain English is a style of writing that conveys your message in the simplest and shortest way possible. It allows the reader to concentrate on the message instead of being distracted by complicated language.

    Some points to keep in mind are:

    - keep sentences short (approximately 10–20 words)
    - use one idea per sentence
    - avoid technical jargon
    - write coherently by structuring content logically and linking ideas smoothly
    - check spelling, punctuation and grammar

- **Use attention-grabbing headlines and hooks**

    Use thought-provoking headlines and hooks that contain a benefit, identify the reader's main needs or concerns or ask a question.

Write a book

Becoming a published author of a book will elevate your personal brand and authority status within your industry category better than any other type of publishing. This is because most people recognise that writing a book is a big achievement. Not only because it contains your valuable content - your stories, perspectives, ideas, methods, case studies, models and learnings - but also because it takes dedication and persistence.

One of the primary reasons of writing a book is for brand positioning. The harsh reality is that you probably won't sell many books, but the fact that you've written a book speaks volumes.

You can use the term 'author' in your bio, on your LinkedIn profile or in your résumé. You can give your book away at workshops, as a Christmas gift to clients, as a door prize or just send it to someone you just met at a networking event. You can also use your book to leverage publicity opportunities. The media will often seek out people who have written a book as they are considered subject matter experts who can potentially provide informative commentary for their story.

There are many kinds of books, so the first thing is to be clear on the type of book you want to write. For instance, it could be a book on your thought leadership, a guide or handbook, an anthology (a collection of selected writings by various authors) or a book of interviews.

A book is usually between 25,000 and 50,000 words but can also be much less, depending on the purpose and style. If you don't think you could write that much, consider contributing a chapter in a book as part of an anthology. I know many people who have written chapters for books, and they have been wonderful promotional opportunities for their personal brand.

Nowadays, there are many book coaches who can help you plan and write your book, provide feedback on the manuscript and keep you on track throughout the process. Some coaches can also help you publish and promote your book. There are many publishing options available so it's a good idea to speak with someone who's been there and done that to save you time and effort.

Other publishing opportunities

Here are some other publishing opportunities you can use to build your personal brand credibility and visibility:

- A website in your name that includes your personal bio, value proposition, certifications, qualifications, awards, showreel and speaking or interview videos, affiliations, publications.
- A regular e-newsletter that includes inspirational and educational content sent to a subscriber list.
- A whitepaper, an in-depth and authoritative report on a specific topic related to your area of expertise that presents a problem and provides a solution.
- Handbooks, guides and templates, which can be useful downloads from your website.

Publicity

If you don't think you've got a book in you, having an article or opinion piece published in a newspaper or magazine, being interviewed on a podcast, radio or television, are also potent ways to build your professional profile.

Gift your brand the power of free earned media

When people see positive media coverage, they may talk about 'getting good PR', but they mean good publicity.

PR, or public relations, is the not the same as publicity. Understanding the distinctions between them is helpful when seeking the services of professionals offering different services.

Public Relations is a strategic management function, encompassing a diverse range of communication processes and activities designed to build mutually-beneficial relationships, enhance public profile and manage reputation. Publicity, however, is a tactic of a public relations program designed to generate free media coverage in the mass media or a specialist publication, for example.

In the vast digital landscape and 24/7 news cycle of today, reputations can't be taken for granted and trust with stakeholders can't be assumed. That's why having a strong public relations capability, with a good understanding of how to manage the media and generate free publicity for your brand, is an essential part of running a successful business today.

Types of media

Media can be segmented by content type. The three main types of media content are:

- **Owned media** – content you create, such as your website, blog, social media posts, brochure newsletter, LinkedIn profile, webinars, media releases, articles, opinion pieces, podcasts (yours).
- **Bought media** – content you buy, such as display ads, advertorials, pay per click, boosted content, retargeting, sponsorships, trade shows, paid influencers.
- **Earned media** – content about you that you didn't create or pay for, such as testimonials, reviews, social likes and shares, brand mentions, media coverages such as published articles and editorial, podcasts (others).

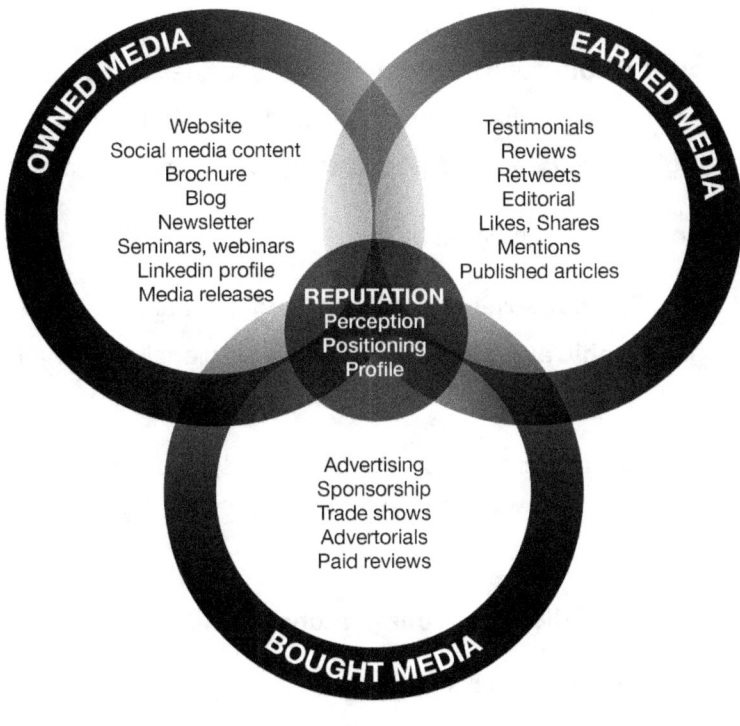

Owned, bought and earned media model

Publicity, in the form of a published article or podcast interview for example, is also earned media. Publicity, as earned media, is more powerful than owned media (a blog) or bought media (a paid ad).

Publicity content about you created or carried by a third party is more credible because it doesn't seem like self-promotion. That's why testimonials – as earned content – are used by businesses because someone singing your praises is more believable than you doing it yourself.

Media can be segmented by format:

- **print media**, such as newspapers, magazines and journals
- **broadcast media**, such as radio and television
- **digital media**, such as podcasts, enewsletters and emagazines.

Media can also be segmented by audience:

- **specific industries** or **topics** for targeted audiences
- **geographic audiences**, such as local, regional, state, national or international mediums for mass audiences.

Using the media to increase your visibility is only effective when you target the right media with the right message for the right audience at the right time.

Why generate publicity for your personal brand?

Publicity is highly effective in building your profile and driving a positive reputation, because it elevates the perception, positioning and profile of your personal brand:

- **Perception** – the credibility and trustworthiness of your personal brand based on what people think and feel. By generously sharing your insights and ideas, you'll build a loyal following over time.
- **Positioning** – the distinguishability of your personal brand compared to competitor alternatives. By sharing what makes you different, including what you stand for as a brand and the difference you seek to make in the world, you can position yourself as a brand of choice.
- **Profile** – the awareness and reach of your personal brand in the marketplace. By sharing your message regularly and consistently across platforms, including in the media, you'll become known for the value you bring and the problem you solve.

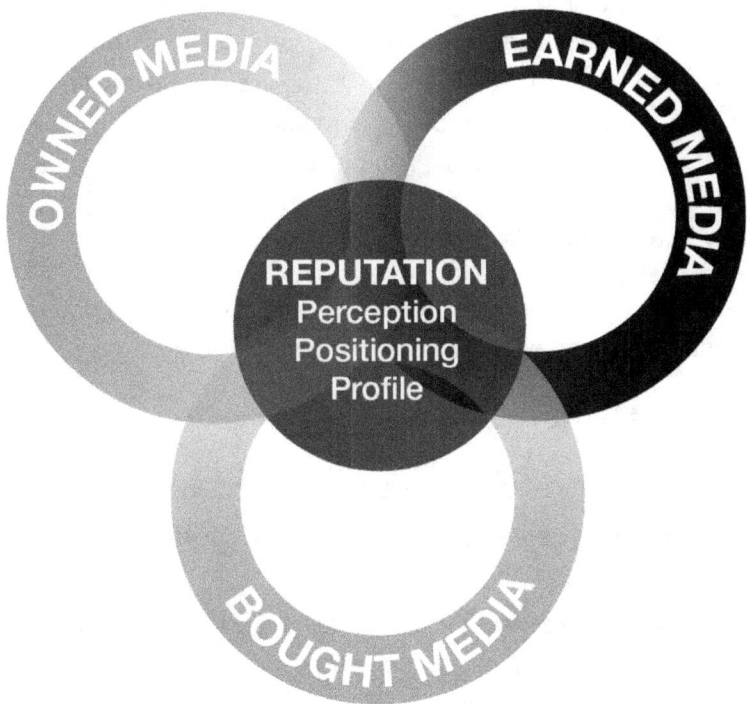

©Ros Weadman

Publicity can also generate leads for your business. Most people are walking around in a state of 'latent purchase readiness' just waiting for the right moment to buy something. They may have done their research but not yet made up their mind. Seeing your published article or listening to your podcast interview just might help them take that next step.

Media relations is a business relationship

Good publicity is most often an outcome of good media relations. And like any business relationship, a relationship with a journalist, editor or producer must be nurtured, needs and expectations met, and a mutually-beneficial value exchange transacted.

In the case of publicity, the value exchange is your NEWSworthy content (story idea/words, interview, images, video) for potential published space or airtime. And while there are no guarantees when it comes to publicity, understanding the media and satisfying its needs, can vastly increase your chances of being successful.

The key is to think NEWSworthy!

What's worth a journalist's or producer's time to publish your story rather than someone else's? Being NEWSworthy, that's what!

Here are some NEWSworthy ideas for your personal brand:

- **Awards** – industry, product or council business awards
- **Something new** – something innovative within your niche or industry
- **Thought leadership** – educating an audience by sharing your deep insights into a particular topic
- **A book** – for a specific audience
- **Opinion piece** – expressing an opinion, usually controversial or provocative, on a specific topic
- **How to** – giving advice, detailing the steps, providing a framework, outlining a process
- **Events** – promoting events such as open days, new product launches, celebrating national days
- **Something different** – think 'man bites dog' instead of 'dog bites man'
- **Case study** – profile a customer's great achievements

How to leverage your publicity

Once you've published an article or been interviewed on a podcast, leverage the publicity by sharing it among your network and on your social media sites.

Here are 9 ways to leverage your earned publicity:

1. Set up a newsroom in your website menu and add all media releases and published articles
2. Create a media kit that includes your bio, list of your published articles, speaking topics, photos of you speaking
3. Create an 'In the Media' panel on your website and add logos with links to the articles
4. Encourage your networks to comment and share your articles
5. Repurpose the article as a newsletter article or as smaller social media posts
6. Embed links to articles in your enewsletter and media releases
7. Update your LinkedIn profile
8. Update your bio
9. Use media logos on marketing materials

One final point on publicity. Remember, it's actually not about you. It's about your audience, or more precisely, the audience of the media. Media outlets are businesses too so they will only publish content that will appeal to their audience.

Activity – Every brand has a story worth telling. What's yours?

Write down five NEWSworthy story ideas that you could turn into a publicity opportunity.

Profitability – Monetise your brand

Commercialise your personal brand by leveraging your thought leadership and intellectual property so you can advance your career to greater heights and grow your business with steady momentum.

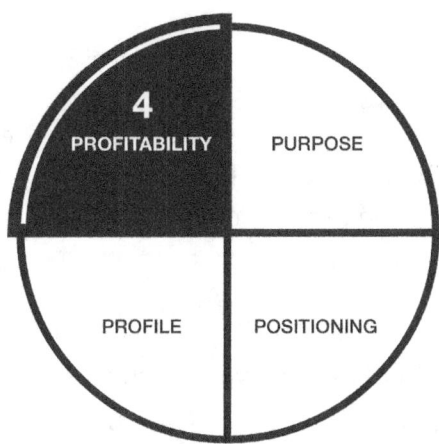

Step 7: Velocity – Accelerate your momentum

> 'When you're that successful, things have momentum, and at a certain point you can't really tell whether you have created the momentum or it's creating you.'
> Annie Lennox, Scottish singer-songwriter

In the dynamic and competitive marketplace, momentum plays a crucial role in driving career or business success and growth. Momentum is about putting in place systems, processes and product ecosystems that create and support a positive and sustained trajectory towards the achievement of goals, improvement of financial performance and enhancement of brand reputation.

Products

One of the key ways of building momentum as a personal brand is to package your intellectual property into a product ecosystem that meets different customer needs and scales your business. Your products are the suite of signature services, programs and events you offer, designed to meet customer needs at different stages of the customer journey.

Core product structure

The below five elements provide a basic structure for designing, delivering and marketing each of your core products, such as a new coaching program or event:

1. **Market** – the target market
2. **Message** – the name and value proposition
3. **Methodology** – the philosophical approach
4. **Mode** – the means of delivery
5. **Marketing Mix** – the price, placement and promotional mediums to attract prospective clients

The model on the next page shows these five elements as a process, starting with identifying the target market for the product through to marketing the product.

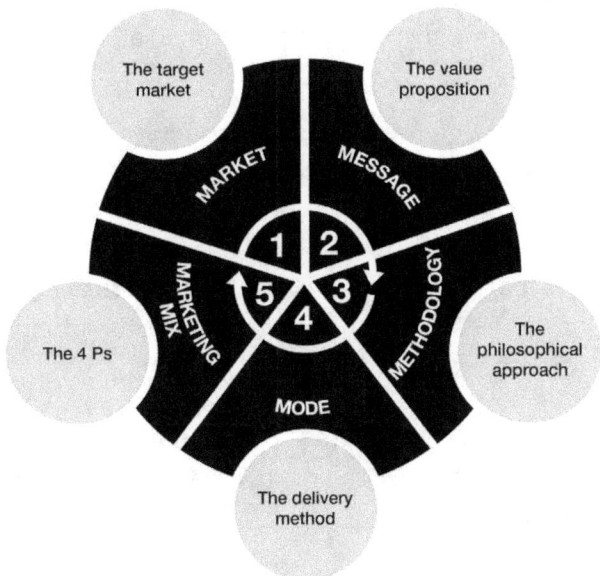

Core Product Structure Model ©Ros Weadman

Step 1: Market

A market is a congregation of people who need to find a solution to their problem. For example, if you're a Pilates instructor, your market could be women aged 30 - 50 years looking to improve their body tone and flexibility so they can lead a more active lifestyle. If you're a leadership coach, your market could be middle managers in large organisations who need to improve their team's performance so they deliver projects more effectively. If you're a financial coach, your market could be owners of small businesses who need help with budgeting so they can run a more profitable business.

Step 2: Message

The message includes both the name of the product and the value proposition. The name of a product is a powerful positioning strategy and can help your product cut through the clutter of the distracted marketplace. The product name can be one or two words, a phrase or have two levels of headings. For example, a short primary word or phrase that denotes the outcome and a short phrase that includes the target market so they can identify with it immediately.

For example:

- INNER BRILLIANCE – personal branding for female executives, entrepreneurs and experts

When choosing a name for your product, do some research to ensure you are not using the same name as a competitor or infringing on someone else's intellectual property.

In the section on 'Value', we created an overarching value proposition for your personal brand. Now it's time to create value propositions for your individual products.

Like your personal brand value proposition, product value propostions need to address the logical and emotional elements of the outcome you achieve for your customer.

So, we're going to create two value propositions for each product – one encompassing the logical or tangible outcomes, such as performance, productivity and revenue; and one encompassing the emotional or intangible outcomes, such as confidence, trust, respect, engagement.

Below is an example of logical and emotional value propositions for my personal branding program.

Product name: *Inner Brilliance Personal Branding™ Program for Women in Small Business*

Logical/tangible: *7 steps to becoming a credible and trusted authority in your industry*

Emotional/intangible: *Gain clarity and confidence to put yourself out there and leave your mark on the world.*

Step 3: Methodology

Your signature methodology or philosophical approach to service delivery is what sets one professional service provider from another. As an example, the Inner Brilliance methodology outlined in this book is my philosophical approach to personal branding. I have created other methodologies for other products (programs and events). By creating your own signature methodology or approach to service delivery, you provide a strategic pathway for clients to navigate from where they are now to where they want to be in the future.

Step 4: Mode

Products can be delivered through various modes of delivery, such as consulting/advisory, one-on-one or one-to-many training, coaching and mentoring, and face-to-face, online or a mixture of both.

Step 5: Marketing Mix

The marketing mix strategies you select are designed to best position you or your products and services in the marketplace and influence your prospective customers to choose your over someone else. Each of your products or services requires its own marketing mix strategies that relate to its specific target market.

Commonly known as the 4Ps, the marketing mix includes *product*, *price*, *promotion* and *placement*. These Ps work together to create the best response from a particular target market to a specific product or service. Other Ps that make up the marketing mix can include *people* - the staff and suppliers involved in getting the product to market; *processes* - the procedures for handling customer enquiries and customer complaints, and after-sales service; *packaging* - the materials used, colours and messages on the packaging; and *production* - the process to develop the product or service. The process directly affects price and timeframe; for example, inefficient productivity can lead to higher prices and a delay in delivery.

The challenge and opportunity for personal brands is to design a marketing mix that delivers a great experience for people from first contact through to the sales process, product/service delivery and after sales support.

Product ecosystem

Once you understand your target market's need to be fulfilled or problem to be solved, you need to match your product to it. This may be one product or it may be a suite of similar products but at different price points to allow a greater portion of the market to use the product.

One way of meeting the needs of several target markets is by creating a product ecosystem. A product ecosystem is a network or mix of different products and services that complement each other and work together to optimise the value exchange in every customer relationship.

Product ecosystems often begin with a core product from which other products are developed. In other words, you take the core product as a basis and create other products that meet the needs of different markets.

For example, a 12-chapter book may be the core product. This book can be turned into a 12-week online training program, with each chapter provided in digital, audio and video formats, all of which can be leveraged as mini products. One person may prefer reading the book, another person may prefer to do the online course, and another may prefer the bite-size chunks of information via podcast or video.

A product funnel is one way to develop a product ecosystem. A product funnel takes your customer on a journey by offering a series of products or services that increasingly meet their needs at a more intense level and with a correspondingly higher price for each level.

Start with the entry to the funnel, the place where prospects get to know you by downloading a free piece of information, usually in exchange for their basic online contact details (first name and email address). Each new level of the funnel introduces a value offering at a higher price point. The pinnacle of the funnel is your most expensive product that generates the highest amount of income. If you are a service business, your most expensive product could, in fact, be you!

The diagram below provides an example of a four-level product funnel for a consultant that takes a person from being a prospect to a customer.

Sample product funnel

Funnel point	Value hierarchy	Product offering examples	Price
Entry of funnel	Free offer	Free downloadable PDF - quiz, self-assessment tool, whitepaper, checklist, ebook Free discovery discussion Free strategy session	Free
Low point of funnel	Low-cost offer	Silver - Package of 1-3 coaching sessions	$low
Mid-point of funnel	Medium-cost offer	Gold - Package of 6 coaching sessions plus resources	$medium
Top of funnel	Most exclusive offer	Platinum - VIP program This is your most exclusive signature product to work directly with you over a longer period of time to achieve maximum results. It could be a retainer model or set period, such as 3, 6 or 12 months.	$premium

> **Activity: create a product ecosystem**
>
> Create a four-level product funnel with:
>
> 1. Free downloadable product
>
> _____
>
> _____
>
> 2. Low-cost offer
>
> _____
>
> _____
>
> 3. Medium-cost offer
>
> _____
>
> _____
>
> 4. Most exclusive offer
>
> _____
>
> _____

Partnerships

When I first entered the consulting world in 2011, I learned quickly that drawing on my vast network of former bosses, workmates and industry peers was crucial to my success in those first few years of business. Having left my job, which I knew back to front, and launching myself into business in which I knew nothing, was a blind leap of faith when I think about it. The harsh reality of going from having a regular fortnightly wage to having no client base and no idea about how to prospect and nurture leads was completely foreign to me.

This is where my networks proved invaluable. Not only did I get my first few jobs from people who I knew in the industry but fast forward over a decade and my networks continue to be a critical part of my business success. Not only for bouncing ideas and coffee catch-ups but also for referring potential clients and establishing strategic alliances.

The wonderful thing about building strong business networks and strategic partners over time is that there is a deep level of trust. This trust extends to all areas of the business relationship. From trusting the quality of their work, trusting that they'll do what they say they're going to do, trusting that they'll represent your brand well and trusting that they've always got your back.

You simply cannot buy trust. It must be earned by nurturing relationships over time. There are several people I've worked with now for over 30 years – writers, designers, photographers and other communications professionals. I trust them implicitly and I know I'll call upon them until the day I retire, and probably beyond.

Over the years I've expanded my network of trusted business confidantes and contacts through building a wonderful client base, meeting new people at networking meetings and conferences, joining business groups, undertaking study, engaging mentors and coaches, and by being part of some of the most inspiring business communities in the world.

There are many ways you can create mutually-beneficial business opportunities through strategic partnerships, such as:

- **Affiliate partnerships** – partners promote your products, books and other resources in exchange for a commission.
- **Referral partnerships** – partners refer their clients or warm leads to you. This can be through a structured referral-based business group like BNI® (Business Networking International) or a more casual arrangement between two business associates.

- **Strategic service partnerships** – partners combine services or collaborate on a project to deliver a more holistic solution to the client.
- **Product development partnerships** – individuals combine their knowledge, expertise and other resources to create a new product or program.
- **Investor partnerships** – a financial partner join forces to get a product or business off the ground.

There's a wonderful African proverb I heard some years ago and to this day I consider it one of the best pieces of wisdom I've learned about valuing relationships: *If you want to go fast go alone; it you want to go far go together.*

The other great thing about having a trusted circle of peers and associates is the ability to get honest feedback and good advice on all sorts of topics at any time. A colleague of mine who I've worked with in various guises for more than 30 years is someone I call regularly to bounce off ideas or to get an alternative perspective. This person knows me well and I highly value their opinion. It doesn't mean I always take their advice but it's great to have a different point of view to consider.

Some words on trust

Entering any partnership is a big decision, no matter the length or substance of the contract. It requires a level of trust by each party: 'contractual trust', which is faith that the obligations of the contract will be met; and 'relationship trust', which extends beyond the tangibles of the contract. It's a commitment by both parties to nurture the health of the relationship, being honest and transparent, following through on promises, not speaking badly about the other party when they're not in the room, and each doing all in their power to stay aligned with, and act towards, the achievement of the big picture goals and desired outcomes.

Activity – list your potential partners

Make a list of people in your network who could be potential partners for:

- Bouncing off ideas

_____

_____

- Seeking feedback or an alternative perspective

_____

_____

- Referring potential clients

_____

_____

- Collaborating with on a project

_____

_____

- Any other purpose where there is a mutually-beneficial outcome

_____

_____

Step 8: Viability – Secure your success

> *'Always be yourself, express yourself, have faith in yourself, do not go out and look for a successful personality and duplicate it.'*
> Bruce Lee, master of martial arts, actor and filmmaker

Building a personal brand is not a set and forget process; it's a work in progress as individuals expand their knowledge, broaden their experiences and evolve their career goals. Beyond the strategic components of defining, marketing and monetising your personal brand, you also need strategies to manage and protect your personal brand for long-term success.

Psychology

Ultimate success formula

Earlier in the book I talked about personal branding starting with intention and the need to adopt a personal brand mindset. But sometimes, you need some structure or guidance to help get you in the right frame of mind and to stay on track. World-renowned life coach, Anthony Robbins, recommends a four-step process for achieving any result you want in life and it all starts with mindset.

Robbins' calls this framework the 'Ultimate Success Formula'[30], which includes:

1. Decide on the outcome you want to achieve by building a personal brand
2. Take massive action towards this outcome
3. Notice what's working or not working along the journey
4. Continue to change your strategic approach to stay on track.

With research clearly showing that a person's physiology can impact their mindset, I suggest adding a fifth step to the formula:

5. Create a physiology that supports success

1. Decide on your outcome

Knowing what you are aiming for is fundamental to business success. If you want to be in control of the results you are getting in business, you need to have clarity about the specific goal that you want to achieve. Once you know what outcome you are looking for, you then need to focus on it.

Consider these questions to help decide on the outcome you want:

- Where do I want to be in my career in five years? in 10 years? In 20 years?
- How will I know when I've achieved my outcome?
- What will success look like? sound like? feel like?
- What will my typical day, week, month or year look like?
- Where will I be living?

2. Take massive action

Make decisions

Taking massive action means making decisions and lots of them. The word 'cide', in latin, means 'cut', as in cut off. Therefore, to decide something means to cut off from something. Tony Robbins says 'Making a true decision means committing to achieving a result, and then cutting yourself off from any other possibility'.[31]

Robbins believes there are three decisions[32] we make every moment that control our destiny:

1. Your decision about **what to focus on**

2. Your decisions about **what things mean to you**
3. Your decisions about **what to do** to create the results you want.

When you decide to take control of your personal brand and pursue the career success of your dreams, you will be more inspired to move away from people, places and projects that don't light you up, and move towards people, places and projects that give you more purpose, meaning and fulfilment.

Embrace uncertainty

You may feel a little uneasy when first starting out to share your ideas and insights online, speak up more in team meetings or go for higher paid positions. However, once you get clear on your values, purpose, vision and value through the personal branding process, you will be better equipped to embrace the uncertainty of stepping out of your comfort zone. You will feel more confident to put yourself out there because you have more clarity on what you stand for, more conviction of your principles and more certainty about where you're heading in the future.

Facilitate change

For many people, taking steps outside of your comfort zone to build a strong personal brand is daunting. But like anything in life, if you are feeling any dissatisfaction, pain or problem around your current situation, that's a sure sign that change is not only desirable but inevitable; it's just a matter of when the person will finally take that first step. At some point, there will be a trigger that sets in motion a set of actions to move from the current situation to the desired situation.

The Beckhard-Harris Change Model[33] (D x V x F > R) proposes that for successful change, the combination of a person's dissatisfaction (D) with the status quo / current state, vision (V) of what's possible in the future and having a plan to take first steps (F) in the direction of the vision, must be stronger than the resistance (R) to change. The model provides a simple and useful formula for assessing whether the conditions necessary for change to occur are present. Having a personal brand plan will facilitate the change process and help you achieve the professional success you desire.

3. Notice what's working or not working

This is about applying sensory acuity — using the information taken in through the five senses of vision, hearing, taste, smell and touch (and feel, also known as kinaesthetic) — to determine whether you are getting the results you want from the actions you are currently taking.

Being sensory aware gives you the opportunity to change your focus and take a different action if what you are currently doing is not working.

Consider these questions to help you use sensory acuity to understand what's happening in your professional life:

- What am I seeing on a daily basis that tells me standards are or are not being met?
- What are customers saying about the service they are receiving?
- What feedback am I hearing from my colleagues?
- What am I feeling about the work I'm doing right now?
- Are my thoughts, words and actions aligned with my personal brand?

4. Adjust your strategic approach

Albert Einstein said that the definition of insanity is doing the same thing over and over and expecting a different result. If, through your sensory acuity, you can see / hear / feel you are not getting the results you want, you need to adjust your approach and do something different.

Apply a mindset for success philosophy when adjusting your approach. For example, what if you had a belief that there is no such thing as failure, only feedback? This kind of thinking gives you permission to try new things, view trial and error as a natural part of the process, and move out of your comfort zone, one step at a time.

Consider these questions to help you adjust your approach:

- What's one thing I could do differently to get a different result?
- What have others done who have achieved the same level of success I want to achieve?
- Who in my network can I learn from?
- What are the mindset characteristics of others who have achieved success?

5. Adopt a posture of intent

Having a posture of intent is another positive way of creating a physiology of excellence.

'Our bodies change our minds, our minds change our behaviour and our behaviour changes our outcomes'.[34]

This comes from the research of social psychologist Amy Cuddy who found that physiology does indeed affect the way we think and, therefore, how we behave.

Amy's research shows that our body language not only affects how others see us, but it may also change how we see ourselves. 'Power posing' — standing in a posture of confidence, even when we don't feel confident — can impact our chances of success.

In her research with fellow psychologists Dany Carney and Andy Yap, they noted that two nonverbal body language dimensions are typically linked to high or low power. These are expansiveness (the amount of space that one's body takes up) and openness (degree to which limbs are open or closed). High-power people assume expansive, open postures and low-power people assume constricted and closed postures.

In their study, they found that people asked to assume a high-power pose were found to have elevated testosterone levels (a hormone related to dominance) and lower cortisone levels (a hormone related to stress). This research shows how adopting a posture of intent, in this case, a power pose, can indeed impact a person's psychology and physiology.

Protection

Reputation management is an important part of protecting your personal brand.

The internet has heightened reputational risk for personal brands because of the speed at which reputational damage can occur with bad reviews, news and views spreading like wildfire. That's why it's important for personal brands to not just respond in times of reputational crises but to also prepare for such events before they happen.

Five-point plan for protecting your reputation

1. **Prioritise communication**

    Most people would consider that communication is a given at work and in business, but it's amazing how many people don't prioritise it as part of their modus operandi. Did you know you are communicating even when you're not? Every phone call you don't return, every email you don't respond to, every update you don't give is sending a reputation-defining message to your colleagues or your customers.

    In communication, the small things can have the biggest impact. Communicating your gratitude, such as saying 'thank you' or communicating your acknowledgment of thanks with 'you're welcome' can have a huge positive ripple effect. Not only does it feel good to say these once-common-but-not-so-common courtesies, it also leaves a good impression, fosters trust and nurtures relationships.

2. **Be proactive**

   In the 24/7 global marketplace, reputation management for some, has become an online practice of burying bad reviews and swamping the internet with positive content to 'magically' restore a good name. This approach is one-dimensional, reactive and superficial, and fails to recognise that reputation management is more holistic, complex and authentic than simply 'cleaning up' an online profile.

   Instead, get on the front foot by being proactive. When reputation is as risk of being damaged or is in the process of being damaged, the priority is to restore trust and that starts with communication. If you try to hide and ignore the problem, it won't go away, it will only get bigger. Because when there is no communication an information vacuum occurs, leaving it open for people to make their own assumptions about whether you're guilty or not guilty and this only further diminishes trust and reputation.

   When things do go awry with a client, project or on social media for example, you need to be open with your communication by saying what you know and don't know, show empathy to those impacted, say sorry if an apology is warranted and give people confidence that you're committed to rectifying the problem as soon as possible.

3. **Use disclaimers**

   For professional resources, such as training guides, handbooks, manuals and books, it's a good idea to use a disclaimer that gives no assurances of specific outcomes to the reader and that people should always seek professional advice.

As an example, I use the following statement in my training manuals: 'Each organisation is unique and specific results are based on many factors including the decisions and skills of individuals, resources available, and organisational priorities and practices. As such, no assurance as to specific outcomes can be guaranteed because of using this handbook.'

4. **Trademark your intellectual property**

    Many personal brands develop a suite of brand identity assets such as a logo, tagline and symbols. Through thought leadership and content development they also create models, methodologies, infographics, illustrations and other signature content. If you have developed original materials, it is wise to seek legal advice about protection to prevent another person or entity using your work for their commercial gain.

5. **Take control of your social media**

    Creating boundaries and rules for your online content and presence is essential, especially if you have others in your team who have administration rights to your social media accounts. Some ways to protect your personal brand online include creating a social media policy that defines brand and editorial guidelines, approve all posts before they are scheduled, take unresolved complaints offline and only post 'brand-relevant' content that focuses on the value you provide or leads the industry conversation.

Part 5

THE END ... OR IS IT?

'My will shall shape the future. Whether I fail or succeed shall be no man's doing but my own. I am the force; I can clear any obstacle before me or I can be lost in the maze. My choice; my responsibility; win or lose, only I hold the key to my destiny.'
Elaine Maxwell, author

While we are not born with a manual for living, we each have an inner well of resources – such as curiosity, optimism, persistence and resilience. We draw from this well when we are driven to learn, grow and become better versions of ourselves. The personal branding process taps into this well to access your Inner Brilliance to achieve your career goals and business ambitions.

Like many hero journey stories in the movies, many of which I have highlighted in this book, the first movie ends with the feeling there's likely to be a sequel. Just like the *Star Wars* series, the *Rocky* series, the *Harry Potter* series or the *Karate Kid* series. It's the same with personal branding. The process is ever-evolving and your story will continue to change as you learn and grow, personally and professionally.

PS – It's only the beginning!

Just like Dorothy in the *Wizard of Oz* and *Luke in Star Wars*, you can find and unleash the Inner Brilliance superpower within you.

So, it's over to you. You get to write the next chapter of your professional life because now you know how to tap into your abundant reserve of Inner Brilliance.

I invite you to stay in touch with me and share your story. I'd love to know if this book has helped you in your career or business journey. And by sharing your story of Inner Brilliance you will inspire others to do the same.

To your Inner Brilliance!

ENDNOTES

1. Waller, T. *Personal Brand Management*, Springer Nature Switzerland AG 2020, p. 8

2. Scheidt, Stefan & Henseler, Jörg. Personal branding: A review on a contemporary phenomenon. Conference Paper, 7th DERMARKENTAG, September 27-28, 2018, p. 9

3. Gorbatov S, Khapova SN, Lysova EI. Get Noticed to Get Ahead: The Impact of Personal Branding on Career Success. *Front Psychol*. 2019 Dec 9;10:2662. doi: 10.3389/fpsyg.2019.02662. PMID: 31920774; PMCID: PMC6913621.

4. Hilgard, E., Atkinson, RL, Atkinson, RC. *Introduction to Psychology*, Harcourt Brace Jovanovich, Inc, 1979, p. 91.

5. Kay, K & Shipman, C. *The Confidence Code*, HarperCollins, USA, 2014, p. 50

6. Kay, K & Shipman, C. *The Confidence Code*, p. 78

7. Virgin website, https://www.virgin.com/branson-family/richard-branson-blog/my-top-10-quotes-branding, accessed 26 August 2023.

8. Gary Vaynerchuk, https://www.linkedin.com/posts/garyvaynerchuk_your-personal-brand-is-your-reputation-and-activity-6934910969902993409-K5_-/?trk=public_profile_like_view, accessed 26 August 2023.

9. Gaines-Ross, L. *What Executives Value in Their CEOs*, Harvard Business Review, 2015.

10. Cision PR Newswire website, https://www.prnewswire.com/news-releases/more-than-half-of-employers-have-found-content-on-social-media-that-caused-them-not-to-hire-a-candidate-

according-to-recent-careerbuilder-survey-300694437.html, accessed 28 August 2023.

11. Harvard Business Review, *The Business Case for Purpose*, Harvard Business School Publishing, 2015. https://assets.ey.com/content/dam/ey-sites/ey-com/en_gl/topics/digital/ey-the-business-case-for-purpose.pdf, accessed 26 August 2023.

12. Absolutely Farelly, https://absolutelyfarrelly.com/, accessed 26 August 2023.

13. Joseph Campbell Foundation, https://jcf.org/about-joseph-campbell/, accessed 26 August 2023.

14. Dooley, R. *Brainfluence: 100 ways to persuade and convince consumers with neuromarketing*, John Wiley & Sons, Inc, USA, p. 64.

15. pwc, *Putting Purpose to Work: A study of purpose in the workplace*, 2016 https://www.pwc.com/us/en/about-us/corporate-responsibility/assets/pwc-putting-purpose-to-work-purpose-survey-report.pdf, accessed, 26 August 2023.

16. Collins, J. *Good to Great: Why some companies take the leap…and others don't*, Random House, London 2001, p. 95

17. Collins, J. *Good to Great*, p. 109

18. Madeson, M. Logotherapy: Viktor Frankl's Theory of Meaning, 28 Jul 2020 https://positivepsychology.com/viktor-frankl-logotherapy/, accessed 8 October 2023.

19. Patagonia website, https://www.patagonia.com/ownership/, accessed 26 August 2023.

20. Virgin website, https://www.virgin.com/about-virgin, accessed 26 August 2023.

21. Salesforce website, https://www.salesforce.com/au/events/worldtour/syd19/equality/, accessed 16 August 2023.

22. L&D Picturesque Painting website https://www.ldpp.com.au/about, accessed 26 August 2023
23. TED website, How great leaders inspire action, Sinek, S. https://www.ted.com/talks/simon_sinek_how_great_leaders_inspire_action?language=en, accessed 26 August 2023.
24. United Nations website, https://sdgs.un.org/goals, accessed 26 August 2023.
25. Collins, J. *Good to Great*, p. 195
26. Branson, R. *Screw it, Let's Do it: Lessons in Life*, Random House Australia, 2006.
27. Cialdini, R, *Influence: The psychology of persuasion*, HarperCollins, New York, 2007.
28. Waller, T. *Personal Brand Management*, Springer Nature Switzerland 2020, p. 74
29. About learning website, https://aboutlearning.com/accessed 17 Oct 2023.
30. Robbins, A. *Awaken the Giant Within*, Simon and Schuster UK, 2001.
31. Robbins, T. *Awaken the Giant Within*, p39.
32. Robbins, T. *Awaken the Giant Within*, p40.
33. Abbas, T. Beckhard and Harris Change Formula Explained March 21, 2023 https://changemanagementinsight.com/beckhard-and-harris-change-formula-explained/, accessed 26 August 2023.
34. TED website, Your body language may shape who you are, Cuddy, A. https://www.ted.com/talks/amy_cuddy_your_body_language_shapes_who_you_are?language=en, accessed 26 August

ABOUT THE AUTHOR

Ros Weadman FPRIA is one of Australia's leading authorities on brand communication and reputation. A multiple award winner with more than four decades' experience in public relations, branding and marketing communications, Ros has helped hundreds of personal, business and government brands to market their value, build their profile and enhance their reputation.

Ros believes that personal brands who are clear on their purpose, vision and values, know the value of their solution and are confident in their message, stand apart in a competitive and commoditised marketplace and cut through the noise.

Ros's specialist problem-solving intelligence is strategic brand alignment.

For corporate brands, this involves aligning corporate culture, communications, customer experience and citizenship so there is consistency of brand across organisational operations, marketing channels and customer touchpoints.

For personal brands, this involves aligning passion, purpose, beliefs, values and expertise with brand voice and strategic market positioning so they stand apart from the competition.

Ros is a Fellow of the Public Relations Institute of Australia, and has won several national and state Institute awards for her campaigns.

You can connect with Ros at www.rosweadman.com or on LinkedIn.

Other books Ros has authored

BrandCode, a strategic marketing guide for small business

Enhance Your Reputation, a practical book on building a credible and trusted brand

www.ingramcontent.com/pod-product-compliance
Lightning Source LLC
Chambersburg PA
CBHW072006290426
44109CB00018B/2145